MOTOR VEHICLE LAW

by

Margaret C. Jasper, Esq.

Oceana's Legal Almanac Series:
Law for the Layperson

1998
Oceana Publications, Inc.
Dobbs Ferry, N.Y.

You may order this or any other Oceana publications by visiting Oceana's Web Site at http://www.oceanalaw.com

ISBN: 0-379-11329-5

Oceana's Legal Almanac Series: Law for the Layperson
ISSN: 1075-7376

Manufactured in the United States of America on acid-free paper.

To My Husband Chris

Your love and support
are my motivation and inspiration

-and-

In memory of my son, Jimmy

ABOUT THE AUTHOR

MARGARET C. JASPER is an attorney engaged in the general practice of law in South Salem, New York, concentrating in the areas of personal injury and entertainment law. Ms. Jasper holds a Juris Doctor degree from Pace University School of Law, White Plains, New York, is a member of the New York and Connecticut bars, and is certified to practice before the United States District Courts for the Southern and Eastern Districts of New York, and the United States Supreme Court.

Ms. Jasper has been appointed to the panel of arbitrators of the American Arbitration Association and the law guardian panel for the Family Court of the State of New York, is a member of the Association of Trial Lawyers of America, and is a New York State licensed real estate broker and member of the Westchester County Board of Realtors, operating as Jasper Real Estate, in South Salem, New York.

Ms. Jasper is the author and general editor of the following legal almanacs: Juvenile Justice and Children's Law; Marriage and Divorce; Estate Planning; The Law of Contracts; The Law of Dispute Resolution; Law for the Small Business Owner; The Law of Personal Injury; Real Estate Law for the Homeowner and Broker; Everyday Legal Forms; Dictionary of Selected Legal Terms; The Law of Medical Malpractice; The Law of Product Liability; The Law of No-Fault Insurance; The Law of Immigration; The Law of Libel and Slander; The Law of Buying and Selling; Elder Law; The Right to Die; AIDS Law; The Law of Obscenity and Pornography; The Law of Child Custody; The Law of Debt Collection; Consumer Rights Law; Bankruptcy Law for the Individual Debtor; Victim's Rights Law; Animal Rights Law; Workers' Compensation Law; Employee Rights in the Workplace; Probate Law; Environmental Law; Labor Law; The Americans with Disabilities Act; The Law of Capital Punishment; Education Law; The Law of Violence Against Women; Landlord-Tenant Law; Insurance Law; Religion and the Law; and Commercial Law.

TABLE OF CONTENTS

INTRODUCTION

This legal almanac discusses the variety of laws that pertain to motor vehicles and their drivers. Traffic violations and their enforcement are set forth, including an overview of common traffic infractions. Chapters specifically focusing on two areas of major concern: speeding and drinking and driving are also examined. The almanac also discusses the criminal justice system as it relates to the victims of accidents and their survivors.

The laws concerning young drivers, including licensing requirements and graduated licensing programs are set forth in this almanac, as well as a discussion of underage drinking and legislation addressing reduced alcohol impairment levels applicable to young drivers.

Legislation aimed at enhancing vehicle safety is explored, including seat belt and child restraint laws, air bag safety, helmet use laws, as well as other vehicular safety features and issues. In addition, the recently enacted Transportation Equity Act, legislation designed to improve highway and traffic safety is examined.

The Appendices provide resource directories, applicable statutes, and other pertinent information and data. The Glossary contains definitions of many of the terms used throughout the almanac.

CHAPTER 1:

TRAFFIC REGULATIONS

In General

Traffic regulations are generally governed by state, city and town ordinances. Most violations of the regulations are *infractions*. A traffic infraction is not a crime, and thus would not subject the offender to imprisonment. It is a civil offense which usually results in the assessment of a fine. Depending on the nature of the offense, the Court may also suspend the driver's license or require the offender to attend some type of defensive driving or traffic safety course. In addition, convictions are generally sent to the state Department of Motor Vehicles and recorded on the driver's record.

Procedure

Many people who receive a ticket admit the violation and pay the required fine. In general, no appearance is necessary. The offender merely signs the ticket and returns it to the Court with payment. If the driver contests the ticket, he or she must appear in Court on the date noted on the ticket. The Court will generally grant an adjournment of the date, at least once, upon request. On the appearance date, the driver enters a plea of not guilty and a trial date is set.

Parking Violations

The most common type of ticket is a parking ticket. Parking tickets are issued for a variety of reasons, such as meter violations, no parking zone violations; blocking a fire hydrant, etc. In general, the person in whose name the car is registered will be required to pay the fine. No appearance is generally required for parking violations, unless the offender is contesting the ticket. The ticket must be returned to the Court with the required fine. If, however, the fine is not paid within the time required, additional fees and penalties may be assessed. If tickets are repeatedly ignored and not paid, the registered owner would be designated a *scofflaw* and his or her car could be impounded.

The Traffic Offender's Rights

Even though a traffic infraction is not a crime, the offender is still entitled to certain rights, including the right to: (i) hire an attorney or elect not to do so; (ii) subpoena witnesses; and (iii) testify or elect not to testify. In addition, the offender is entitled to discover information concerning the state's case, e.g., their witnesses and any evidence they will introduce at trial.

Trial

If the offender contests the ticket, a trial date will be scheduled. The offender usually has the right to a jury trial if timely requested. If a jury trial is not requested, a bench trial—i.e., a trial before the judge—will be held.

Trials are generally held in open court. At trial, the offender—referred to as the defendant—will be given the chance to produce witnesses and other evidence. Unwilling witnesses can be subpoenaed by the Court and required to appear.

Failure to Appear

Offender

Depending on the jurisdiction, failure to appear in Court on a traffic infraction may subject the offender to additional fines and costs, suspension of his or her driver's license and a warrant for the offender's arrest. In order to have the license reinstated, the offender must first pay all fines and costs.

Law Enforcement Officer

If the police officer or other law enforcement officer who issued the ticket fails to appear in Court at the time and date scheduled, the offender may be entitled to have the case dismissed.

Driver's License Points

Drivers are assessed "points" on their driver's license for committing a moving violation—i.e., a traffic infraction incurred while driving, as opposed to a parking violation. The number of points assessed varies according to jurisdiction, however, the more serious infraction generally results in a greater number of points. For example, traveling up to 15 miles over the speed limit may carry a 2 point violation whereas 25 miles over the speed limit may incur a 4 point violation.

If the number of points assessed exceeds the state's maximum within a certain period of time, the driver's license may be suspended. The points generally drop off of one's driving record after a set period of time, e.g. 18 months. In addition, points may be removed earlier if the driver attends an approved driver training course.

Defensive Driving Schools

Depending on the nature of the offense and the offender's record, the Court may require an offender to attend an approved traffic safety course with a defensive driving school.

Habitual Traffic Offender

An individual who accumulates a specified number of traffic convictions within a set period of time may be convicted as a habitual traffic offender, and subjected to suspension of driving privileges.

Non-Residents

More than half of the states are members of a drivers license compact under which they agree to forward each other information concerning convictions or judgments entered in their respective states. For instance, if the offender lives in Illinois, and gets a ticket in Indiana, any convictions obtained in Indiana will be forwarded to Illinois by the Indiana Bureau of Motor Vehicles. The Indiana conviction may be used in actions subsequently brought against the offender in Illinois.

In addition, if the out-of-state driver commits an offense that would subject a resident driver to loss of license, the Court may order the out-of-state driver not to drive on that state's roads.

Misdemeanor Traffic Offenses

Serious traffic offenses are usually *misdemeanors*, not infractions. Misdemeanor traffic offenses are crimes, generally governed by the jurisdiction's criminal code. Operating a motor vehicle while under the influence of alcohol, leaving the scene of an accident, driving with a suspended license, and criminal recklessness are types of misdemeanor traffic offenses, some of which are more fully described below and throughout this almanac.

The penalty for a misdemeanor traffic offense is usually a fine, and depending on the nature and severity of the offense, may include a term of imprisonment. In addition, points are assessed against the driver's record, and the driver's license may be suspended.

If an individual is accused of a misdemeanor traffic offense, he or she must appear in Court on the date and time indicated in the ticket. Failure to appear will result in an arrest warrant being issued. An individual who is charged with a misdemeanor is advised to consult an attorney.

Driving with a Suspended License

While state laws may vary, driving with a suspended license is generally considered a criminal misdemeanor traffic offense. Some states classify this offense as a felony if there are multiple violations.

If the driver commits the offense "knowingly"—i.e., aware of the suspension—he or she generally faces a fine and/or jail time, e.g. 30 or 60 days. A second offense would result in stiffer penalties, and subsequent offenses may result in revocation of the driver's license for a period of time.

In order to be found guilty of driving with a suspended license, the prosecutor must prove the case beyond a reasonable doubt. Thus, to demonstrate that the defendant knowingly drove with a suspended license, the prosecution must show that the driver knew—i.e., received some type of notification—of the suspension.

Although a defendant may plead guilty at any time, he or she has the right to a trial, at which time any defenses against the charge may be asserted.

Reckless Driving

Although speeding may be a component of reckless driving, it is not a necessary element, nor does speeding alone constitute reckless driving. In most jurisdictions, reckless driving is considered more serious than speeding, which is generally treated as a traffic infraction.

The specific elements necessary to prove reckless driving are statutory, thus the reader is advised to check the law of his or her own jurisdiction. In general, such statutes define reckless driving as "driving carelessly and in wanton disregard of the safety of others", or "driving under circumstances showing a reckless disregard of consequences."

Some have argued that reckless driving statutes are unconstitutionally vague, particularly since many of the acts underlying the alleged violation are contained in other statutes, e.g., speeding, running a red light, etc. However, courts have held that the ultimate issue is whether under the totality of the circumstances, the factfinder may find that the defendant consciously drove the vehicle in an unreasonable manner with reckless disregard for the safety of other persons or property.

A reckless driving conviction may result in a suspension or revocation of the driver's license. In addition, a jail sentence or substantial fine may be assessed against the driver.

Failure to Obey Traffic Control Devices

According to the Insurance Institute for Highway Safety, ignoring red lights and disobeying other traffic controls like stop and yield signs is the most frequent reason for what is termed the "urban crash." Researchers studied police accident reports on public roads in four urban areas during 1990 and 1991. Of 13 crash types researchers identified, ignoring traffic controls accounted for 22 percent of all crashes.

Twenty-four percent of such crashes involved running red lights, a particularly dangerous practice. The Institute's study indicated that motorists are more likely to be injured in crashes involving red light running than in other types of crashes. Occupant injuries occurred in 45 percent of those crashes, compared with 30 percent for other types of crashes.

Demographics

According to a study which attempted to profile "red light runners," it was found that, as a group, they are younger, less likely to use safety belts, have poorer driving records, and drive smaller and older vehicles than drivers who obey red light signals. In addition, red light runners are more than three times as likely to have multiple speeding convictions on their driving records. No gender differences were found between violators and those who obeyed the traffic signals.

Red Light Cameras

Because enforcing traffic laws in urban areas is difficult, the "red light camera" has become a popular enforcement device. A red light camera automatically photographs a vehicle whose driver runs a red light. The red light camera system is connected to the traffic signal and to sensors buried in the pavement at the crosswalk. The system continuously monitors the traffic signal. The camera is triggered by any vehicle passing over the sensors above a pre-set minimum speed and specified time after the signal has turned red. A second photograph is taken that typically shows the red light violator in the intersection.

The camera records the date, time of day, time elapsed since the beginning of the red signal, and the speed of the vehicle. The electronic flash produces clear images of vehicles under all light and weather conditions. The cameras typically are set so only those vehicles that enter an intersection after the light has turned red are photographed. Drivers who enter on yellow but are still in the intersection when the light changes to red are not photographed. This technology is intended to catch vehicles driven by motorists who intentionally run red lights.

Trained law enforcement officials review every picture to verify vehicle information and ensure that the vehicle violated the law. Tickets are mailed to vehicle owners only in cases where it's clear the vehicle ran the red light.

Red light cameras do not violate a motorists' privacy, as has been argued. Driving is a regulated activity on public roads. By obtaining a license, motorists agree to abide by certain rules, such as obeying traffic signals. In any event, red light camera systems can be designed to photograph only a vehicle's rear license plate—not vehicle occupants, depending on local laws.

In order for localities to use the cameras for law enforcement purposes, laws must authorize enforcement agencies to cite red light violators by mail. The legislation also must make the vehicle owner responsible for the ticket, establishing a presumption that the registered owner is the vehicle driver at the time of the offense. Violations photographed by red light cameras are most commonly treated in two ways—as traffic violations or as the equivalent of parking tickets, depending on state law.

If, as in New York, red light camera violations are treated like a parking citation, the law can make the registered vehicle owner responsible without regard to who is driving at the time of the offense. Virginia makes red light camera violations a civil offense like New York, but unlike New York, it allows the registered owner to avoid the citation by filing an affidavit that he or she wasn't driving at the time of the violation.

A red light camera costs approximately $50,000. Installation and sensors cost about $5,000. These startup costs can be offset by fines paid by violators, savings from crashes prevented, and by allowing police to focus on other matters. Most importantly, the use of red light cameras has been shown to reduce red light violations and intersection crashes, a benefit which far outweighs the initial cost.

Failure to Maintain Automobile Insurance

All states require an individual who registers a car to purchase automobile liability insurance. Liability coverage indemnifies the insured for the cost of bodily injury and property damage losses sustained by a third party where the insured is determined to be at fault for the accident. The insurance carrier also bears the cost of the insured's legal defense.

Each state sets its own minimum liability insurance requirements. Failure to maintain automobile liability insurance is generally a misdemeanor and subjects the offender to criminal fines and penalties, such as a jail sentence.

A chart of the minimum automobile insurance liability limits by state is set forth at Appendix 1.

Equipment Violations

If an individual receives a ticket for an equipment violation, such as a broken headlight, proof that the violation was fixed since the time the ticket was issued should be presented in Court on the appearance date. A Court will likely dismiss an equipment violation ticket if it is shown that the problem was fixed.

CHAPTER 2:

SPEEDING

Setting Speed Limits

Speed limits are typically set based on the type of road, e.g. a highway versus a two-lane road, and whether the surrounding area is urban, suburban, or rural. Although roadways may be assessed a "design speed"—i.e., the maximum safe speed that can be maintained when conditions on the particular road are optimal—this is not always a safe "travel speed." Because conditions are not always favorable, actual speed limits are set somewhat lower than the design speeds.

History of Speed Limit Laws

Speed limit laws have traditionally been the responsibility of the states. In 1973, due to the oil shortage, Congress directed the U.S. Department of Transportation to withhold highway funding from states that did not adopt a maximum speed limit of 55 mph. As an added bonus, studies indicated that the lower speed limit resulted in a reduction in automobile fatalities on the nation's highways.

Nevertheless, as concerns about fuel availability diminished, speeds started to increase. By the mid-1980s, a substantial majority of vehicles on rural interstates were exceeding the 55 mph limit. In 1987, in response to claims that deaths and injuries would not increase if the limit were raised, made on the basis that drivers were already exceeding that limit, Congress allowed states to increase their speed limits on rural interstates to 65 mph.

In 1995, the maximum speed limit was finally repealed by the National Highway System Designation Act, permitting states to set their own limits for the first time since 1974. Shortly thereafter, many states raised their speed limits on both rural and urban interstates and limited access roads.

According to studies conducted by the Insurance Institute for Highway Safety, the higher speed limits resulted in cars traveling at even higher speeds. For example, in Maryland, which retained 55 mph limits on rural interstates until 1995, monitoring demonstrated that the proportion of cars traveling faster than 70 mph remained virtually unchanged at 7 percent during 1988-93. By 1994, only 12-15 percent of cars were exceeding 70, whereas in neighboring Virginia, which switched to 65 mph limits, the percentage exceeding 70 mph went from 8 percent in 1988 to 29 percent by 1992 and 39 percent by 1994.

A table of state maximum posted speed limits is set forth at Appendix 2.

Automobile Crashes and Speeding

According to the National Highway Traffic Safety Administration (NHTSA), speeding is one of the most commonly reported factors associated with crashes. Speeding reduces the time drivers have to avoid crashes, increases the likelihood of crashing, and contributes to the severity of crashes that do occur. In fact, speed is a factor in 31 percent of all fatal crashes, killing an average of 1,000 Americans every month. NHTSA estimates the economic cost to society of speed-related crashes to be more than $29 billion each year. Health care costs alone are about $4 billion per year.

Speeding is a major factor in failing to avoid an accident because it increases the distance a vehicle travels between the time the driver detects an emergency until the driver reacts, and also increases the distance needed to stop the vehicle once the emergency is perceived.

In a high speed crash, a passenger vehicle is subjected to forces so severe that the vehicle structure cannot withstand the force of the crash. Thus, the vehicle occupants cannot be sufficiently protected from the impact. Further, speeding not only endangers the driver and occupants of the speeding car, but also threatens the safety of other vehicles and pedestrians.

In addition, the performance of automobile safety devices, such as airbags and seat belts, and roadside safety features, such as barriers and rails, are severely compromised in high speed crashes.

Demographics

Although speeding is a problem among all driver age groups, automobile crashes and traffic violations involving young drivers are much more likely to be speed-related as opposed to older drivers. In fact, the motor vehicle crash death rate per 100,000 people is particularly high among 16-24 year-olds.

According to the NHTSA, the relative proportion of speed- related fatal crashes decreases with increasing driver age. About 37 percent of all drivers age 14-19 involved in fatal crashes were in speed-related crashes, as opposed to 7 percent among drivers 70 and up. At all ages, male drivers are more likely than female drivers to be involved in speed-related fatal crashes.

Trucks and Speeding

Large trucks require much longer distances than cars to stop. Lowering speed limits for trucks makes heavy vehicle stopping distances closer to those of lighter vehicles. Slower truck speeds also allow automobile drivers to pass trucks more safely. Crashes involving large trucks not only can cause massive traffic tie-ups in congested areas, but they put other road users at great risk—98 percent of the people killed in two-vehicle crashes involving a passenger vehicle and a large truck are occupants of the passenger vehicles.

Studies have shown that lower speed limits for trucks on 65 mph highways lower the proportion traveling faster than 70 mph without increasing variation among vehicle speeds. In one study, only 4 percent of large trucks exceeded 70 mph on Ohio's rural interstates with 55 mph speed limits for large trucks and 65 for cars, but up to six times the proportion of trucks exceeded 70 mph on rural interstates in three other states with uniform 65 mph speed limits. Another study found that the percentage of trucks going faster than 70 mph was twice as large in states with uniform 65 mph limits.

The human and economic costs of truck crashes weigh heavily on other road users. More than 5,000 people died in 1996 from injuries in crashes involving large trucks, and most were passenger vehicle occupants. Large trucks require much longer distances than cars to stop, even with properly adjusted brakes. Their brakes are more likely to be out of adjustment, compared with cars, and their drivers are often overtired from working long hours—conditions that can magnify the contribution of speed to crashes. Although large trucks accounted for 3 percent of registered vehicles and 7 percent of vehicle miles traveled in 1995, they were involved in 12 percent of passenger vehicle occupant deaths.

Speed Limit Enforcement

For enforcement purposes, police officers must be able to verify vehicle speeds. Methods vary with localities and resources, but most fall under the general types listed below.

Radar

Police radar transmits a microwave signal at a known frequency and then receives the signal that is reflected back from the object. The signal frequency returns to the radar unit in proportion to the speed of the moving vehicle, and the vehicle's speed is displayed. Radar signals also can be used to trigger warning signs that display vehicle speeds to drivers.

Radar is highly reliable and accurate. However, it may be difficult in heavy traffic to pinpoint specific vehicles. Nevertheless, the reliability of radar speed measurements has been repeatedly upheld by the courts.

Radar Detectors

Radar detectors are designed to assist drivers in avoiding speeding tickets. Studies indicate that drivers with radar detectors activate their brake lights suddenly and reduce their speed when suddenly exposed to police radar. Before exposure, vehicles with detectors were traveling significantly faster than those without detectors. By one mile past the radar, more than three-fourths of the vehicles with radar detectors were traveling at least 5 mph faster than the speed limit.

Research indicates that drivers with radar detectors are consistently overrepresented among the fastest speeders. Use of a radar detector demonstrates an intention to speed that distinguishes users of these devices from drivers who speed occasionally or inadvertently. In a survey of users, more than half admitted to driving faster than they would without their radar detectors.

The Federal Highway Administration has prohibited radar detector use in commercial vehicles involved in interstate commerce since January 1994. Radar detectors also are banned in all vehicles in Virginia and the District of Columbia and in big truck rigs in New York and Illinois.

Prior to the ban, studies conducted by the Insurance Institute for Highway Safety measured speeds and radar detector use in trucks in 17 states and found that more than half of all trucks, and half of trucks carrying hazardous materials, were using radar detectors.

States have a legitimate interest in banning the possession and use of radar detectors. Despite claims that prohibiting radar detectors violates numerous constitutional principles, no court has held that radar detector bans, either by statute or regulation, is constitutionally restricted.

In fact, a 1995 U.S. Court of Appeals decision unanimously upheld the federal government ban on radar detector use in commercial vehicles involved in interstate commerce. In its opinion, the court wrote that the Federal Highway Administration "promulgated the rulemaking in order to reduce speeding and thereby reduce the severity of accidents when they occur." It added that, because commercial vehicles "are much larger and heavier than other vehicles, the damage they cause . . . in accidents at excessive speeds is much greater."

Radar Detector-Detectors

A radar detector-detector is an electronic device which can isolate and identify the characteristic microwave radiation emitted by radar detectors. They respond to a nearby radar detector with an audible beep and display that vary with the intensity of the microwave energy detected by the radar detector-detector. These devices can deter speeding by preventing drivers from assuming they can speed with impunity because they have purchased a radar detector.

Photo Radar

Radar signals are used to trigger cameras that photograph speeding vehicles as they pass a specified point. These devices use a low-powered doppler radar speed sensor to detect speeding vehicles. This triggers a motor-driven camera and flash unit which photographs vehicles traveling faster than a set speed. The date, time, and speed are recorded along with a photo. Speed cameras are usually set so they will not be activated unless a vehicle is traveling significantly faster than the posted limit—often 10 mph faster. A visible police presence typically accompanies photo radar in the United States to maximize its deterrent effect. Portable units are placed at the roadside in or near a marked police car, and signs usually announce that photo radar is in use.

Speed cameras have been used for more than 20 years in a number of countries including Australia, Austria, Canada, Germany, Greece, Italy, the Netherlands, Norway, South Africa, Spain, Switzerland, and Taiwan. In Victoria, Australia, speed cameras were introduced in late 1989, and police reported that within three months the number of offenders triggering photo radar decreased by 50 percent. Deaths fell 30 percent in 1990 compared with 1989. The percentage of vehicles significantly exceeding the speed limit decreased from about 20 percent in 1990 to less than 4 percent in 1994.

Lasers

A laser emits a narrow band of light which is transmitted to a targeted vehicle. The light is returned to the laser and displays the speed of the vehicle. These devices are similar in size and weight to police radar, and can accurately isolate individual vehicles. Because laser light cannot be picked up by radar detectors, drivers who have purchased radar detectors to avoid speed law enforcement can no longer assume they can speed undetected. Although detector manufacturers are marketing laser detectors, the narrowness of the laser beam reduces the likelihood that a laser detector will identify the beam in time to provide drivers with enough advance warning to slow down and avoid a ticket.

Vehicle Average Speed Calculator and Recorder (VASCAR)

A VASCAR device consists of a portable computer which accurately clocks, calculates, and displays speed based on the time a vehicle takes to travel a known length of road. VASCAR is passive, providing an average speed measurement over a greater distance than is possible with radar.

VASCAR enables police officers to positively identify speeding vehicles and can be used in various modes, whether from patrol cars following speeders or from cars going in the opposite direction. VASCAR can be useful under conditions where radar is not practical. When used correctly, VASCAR is very reliable. It emits no radiation, so it cannot be picked up by radar detectors.

Aerial Speed Measurement

Like VASCAR, aerial speed measurement is based on visual detection and identification of targeted vehicles. Police in low-flying aircraft measure vehicle speed based on the time it takes to travel between two or more pavement markings. The vehicles are timed over measured distances, usually marked by two parallel lines painted across the road. The police radio the speed information to patrol cars which make the stop. Aerial surveillance can provide very accurate speed measurements and allows police to focus on the fastest speeding vehicles.

Electronic Roadside Signs

Electronic roadside signs are used to display vehicle speeds as the vehicle passes the sign, and warn drivers that they are speeding. Research indicates that mobile roadside speedometers can reduce speeds at the sites of the speedometers as well as for short distances down the road. When used in conjunction with even limited police enforcement, the effect of speedometers is promising.

CHAPTER 3:

DRINKING AND DRIVING

In General

Alcohol impairment is a known contributor to motor vehicle accidents. It is a misconception, however, that one must be "drunk" in order to be a dangerous driver. Many alcohol-impaired drivers do not appear visibly drunk. Studies have indicated that even small amounts of alcohol can impair driving skills.

Another common misbelief is that the likelihood of impairment is contingent on the type of drink. Some mistakenly believe that beer, for instance, is less likely to cause impairment compared to hard liquor. However, impairment is not determined by the type of drink. It is measured by the amount of alcohol ingested over a specific period of time. In fact, beer is the most common drink consumed by people stopped for alcohol-impaired driving or involved in alcohol-related crashes.

Many believe that they have had enough time to "sober up" between the time they drink and the time they drive, and are unaware of how much time is actually needed for one's body to metabolize alcohol. Studies indicate that most people need at least one hour to metabolize one drink.

Due in large part to strong enforcement initiatives and public awareness campaigns, the incidence of alcohol-impaired driving has been reduced in recent years. Nevertheless, as indicated by the following 1996 statistics from the National Highway Traffic Safety Administration (NHTSA), drinking and driving is still a major safety problem:

1. 17,126 people were killed in crashes involving alcohol in the United States—an average of one every 32 minutes. These deaths constituted approximately 41% of the total 41,907 traffic fatalities for the year.

2. Alcohol-related traffic deaths among 15-20 year olds increased for the first time in seven years from 2,206 in 1995 to 2,315 in 1996. The number of alcohol related traffic fatalities involving the same age group with high blood alcohol levels increased.

3. 3,732 alcohol-related traffic fatalities involved drivers at BAC levels under .10—the legal limit in 34 states. This accounts for one-fourth of the total.

4. About 1,058,990 were injured in alcohol-related crashes -an average of one person approximately every 30 seconds.

5. Every weekday night from 10 p.m. to 1 a.m., one in thirteen drivers is drunk—i.e., they have a BAC of .08 or more. Between 1 a.m. and 6 a.m. on weekend mornings, one in seven drivers is drunk.

6. About two in every five Americans will be involved in an alcohol-related crash at some time in their lives.

7. Economic costs of alcohol-related crashes are estimated to be $45 billion yearly.

8. During the period 1982 through 1995, approximately 300,274 persons lost their lives in alcohol-related traffic crashes.

9. In the past decade, four times as many Americans died in drunk driving crashes as were killed in the Vietnam War.

10. Traffic crashes are the greatest single cause of death for every age from five through twenty-seven. Almost half of these crashes are alcohol-related.

Blood Alcohol Concentration (BAC)

The primary indicator of whether a person has had too much to drink is their blood alcohol concentration (BAC). The BAC describes the concentration of alcohol in a person's blood expressed as weight per unit of volume. For example, at 0.10 percent BAC, there is a concentration of 100 mg of alcohol per 100 ml of blood. The term is somewhat misleading because a blood sample is not necessary to determine a person's BAC. It can be measured much more simply by analyzing exhaled breath.

Because the rate that alcohol is absorbed into the blood differs from person to person based on such factors as age, weight and gender, the effect that alcohol will have on a particular person varies greatly. Other factors, such as the amount of food in the stomach, also affect alcohol absorption. Therefore, it is difficult to determine exactly how many drinks will result in a heightened BAC.

The first state laws prohibited driving while intoxicated or while under the influence of alcohol. In practical terms, this meant that only obviously impaired drivers—so-called drunks—were likely to be arrested and, even then, it was difficult to obtain a conviction because no objective standard existed to prove intoxication. When the relationship between BACs and impairment of skills was established, it became possible to define offenses in terms of a BAC above a defined threshold.

Every state law now uses BAC results to prosecute offenders. Initially, this was done through laws that established a rebuttable presumption of impairment at or above a specified BAC. Now 48 states and the District of Columbia have "per se" laws defining the offense as driving with a BAC above a proscribed limit, similar to a speed limit. A "per se" violation needs no further corroboration and the BAC in and of itself is proof that the law was violated. Defendants can no longer try to prove they were not impaired, although they can challenge the validity of the BAC tests.

As an example, the New York DWI statute is set forth at Appendix 3 as a model DWI statute which defines a BAC of 0.10 as a per se driving while intoxicated violation.

Driving with a BAC of 0.10 percent is a crime in 33 states and the District of Columbia, and evidence of an alcohol violation in South Carolina. It is a crime to drive with a BAC of 0.08 percent in 15 states, and an alcohol violation in Massachusetts.

A Table of state DUI/DWI laws is set forth at Appendix 4.

Drinking and Accidents

The likelihood that a driver will have an accident increases steadily at BAC levels higher than zero. Even at a BAC as low as 0.02 percent, alcohol affects driving ability. The probability of a crash begins to increase significantly at 0.05 percent BAC and climbs rapidly after about 0.08 percent.

Although drivers with BACs at or above 0.10 percent represent only 17 percent of all drinking drivers on weekend nights, they represent 87 percent of the fatally injured drivers who had been drinking during those time periods. In fact, studies indicate that for drivers with BACs above 0.15 percent on weekend nights, the likelihood of being killed in a single-vehicle crash is more than 380 times higher than it is for nondrinking drivers.

Although alcohol is known to increase crash likelihood, its presence is neither necessary nor sufficient to cause a crash. Every crash in which a driver has a high BAC is not caused by alcohol. Nevertheless, statistics have demonstrated that a large percentage of drivers who are fatally injured have a BAC of at least 0.10 percent.

According to a 1996 NHTSA study, 32 percent of all traffic deaths occurred in crashes in which at least one driver had a BAC of 0.10 percent or more. The incidence of alcohol involvement is much lower in crashes involving nonfatal injuries, and it is lower still in crashes that do not involve injuries at all.

Demographics

Accidents involving men are much more likely than those involving women to be alcohol-related. Among fatally injured male drivers of passenger vehicles in 1996, 39 percent had BACs of 0.10 percent or more. The corresponding proportion among women was 19 percent. Alcohol involvement is highest for men ages 21-30. Although studies indicate that the percentage of women with high BACs has increased from 1986 to 1996, the increase has not been significant.

Time of Day

Alcohol-related accidents may occur at any time of day, however, the incidence peaks at night and increases on weekends. Among passenger vehicle drivers who are fatally injured between 9 p.m. and 6 a.m., 58 percent have BACs at or above 0.10 percent compared with 21 percent during other hours. Forty-six percent of all fatally injured drivers on weekends—defined as 6 p.m. Friday to 6 a.m. Monday—have BACs of 0.10 percent or more. During the rest of the week, the proportion is twenty-five percent.

According to the NHTSA, the rate of alcohol involvement in fatal crashes is three and one-third times as high at night than as during the day. For all crashes, the alcohol involvement rate is nearly five times as high at night.

Administrative License Suspensions

Among the most effective laws designed to deter drinking and driving are administrative license suspension (ALS) laws. Forty states and the District of Columbia have ALS laws. ALS laws authorize police to confiscate the licenses of drivers who either fail or refuse to take a chemical test for alcohol.

Because administrative licensing action is triggered by failing or refusing to take a chemical test—not by conviction—anyone arrested is immediately subject to suspension. Thus, ALS laws, which apply to both first-time and multiple offenders, remove impaired drivers from the road quickly, and virtually ensure that penalties will be applied.

In the meantime, drivers are given a notice of suspension, which also serves as a temporary permit. Depending on the state, this permit may be valid for 7 to 45 days, during which time the suspension may be appealed. If there is no appeal, or if the appeal is not upheld, the license is suspended for a prescribed period of time.

Effects of Suspension

State laws vary in terms of blood alcohol concentration thresholds, length of time a temporary license is valid, the period within which a hearing must be held, and length of suspension. Suspensions may continue for 7 days to a year for first-time offenders, but most commonly last 90 days. Longer suspensions are specified for repeat violators. It is important to note that ALS laws do not replace criminal prosecution, which is handled separately through the courts.

Longer periods of license suspension may be expected to have stronger effects, while those of short duration may have very limited effects. The NHTSA recommends that ALS laws impose at least a 90-day suspension or a 30-day suspension followed by 60 days of restricted driving.

Some states allow hardship licenses so that offenders may drive to work. Thirty-five states permit some offenders to drive only if their vehicles have been equipped with ignition interlocks. These devices analyze a driver's breath and disable the ignition if the driver has been drinking.

Although many offenders continue to drive after having their licenses suspended, many studies have indicated that the suspensions reduce recidivism compared with offenders whose licenses are not suspended. In addition, the reductions in violations and crashes associated with license suspension continue well beyond the suspension period.

In 20 states, multiple offenders may forfeit vehicles that are driven while impaired by alcohol. Provisions for temporary vehicle impoundment or suspension of vehicle registration or license plates exist in 20 states, and in 9 of these—Florida, Indiana, Maryland, Minnesota, North Dakota, Ohio, South Dakota, Utah, and Virginia—the provisions may apply to first as well as multiple offenders. Some states have provisions for both temporary impoundment and vehicle forfeiture.

Deterrence

The success of laws against alcohol-impaired driving depends largely on deterrence, or keeping potential offenders off the roads in the first place. A well-publicized and enforced ALS law increases public perception that punishment for alcohol-impaired driving is likely to occur and will be swiftly applied and appropriately severe—a perception that is necessary to deter potential offenders.

Constitutional Considerations

Courts have held that although licenses are taken prior to a hearing, due process is provided because ALS laws allow for prompt post-suspension hearings. People whose licenses are suspended have the right to a prompt administrative hearing to determine the validity of the arrest and any alcohol testing.

Defendants have claimed that the double jeopardy clause of the U.S. Constitution prohibits the state from prosecuting an offender whose license has been suspended under ALS. But high courts in several states have found that a criminal prosecution following ALS doesn't violate the double jeopardy clause.

Cost-Benefit Analysis

ALS laws are not costly to enforce. In most states, drivers who have their licenses suspended must pay a reinstatement fee to receive a new license at the end of the suspension period. These fees, which are paid by offenders and not taxpayers, can cover or exceed the cost of the program. In addition, states gain additional funds by qualifying for federal safety incentive grants.

An NHTSA study of three state programs found not only that direct revenues exceeded expenses, but also that state costs associated with nighttime crashes declined dramatically. A study conducted by the Insurance Institute for Highway Safety found that ALS laws reduce the number of drivers involved in fatal crashes by about 9 percent during the high-risk nighttime hours.

Sobriety Checkpoints

Although police cannot stop and test individual drivers without cause, they can investigate any driver who, based on established criteria, appears to have been driving while impaired by alcohol. Most alcohol-impaired driving arrests are made by officers on routine patrol who discern signs of impairment after stopping a driver for an ordinary traffic violation.

Some jurisdictions have their officers working exclusively on enforcing alcohol-related laws. In that connection, they may set up sobriety checkpoints at specified locations to identify impaired drivers. At the sobriety checkpoint, all drivers, or a predetermined proportion of them, are stopped based on rules that prevent police from arbitrarily selecting drivers. Sobriety checkpoints are often established at times when drinking and driving is most prevalent, such as weekends and certain holiday periods.

Checkpoints are a very visible enforcement method intended to deter potential offenders as well as to catch violators. If checkpoints are set up frequently over long enough periods and are well publicized, they are effective deterrents to drivers who fear they will be apprehended if they drink and drive.

The U.S. Supreme Court held in 1990 that properly conducted sobriety checkpoints are legal under the federal Constitution. Most state courts that have addressed the issue have upheld checkpoints, but some have interpreted state law to prohibit checkpoints.

Passive Alcohol Sensors

Passive alcohol sensors identify alcohol in the exhaled breath near a driver's mouth. They are particularly effective in situations where the driver is able to effectively hide symptoms of impairment for short periods of time. Because passive alcohol sensors are not intrusive, they have been held not to violate the constitutional prohibitions against unreasonable search and seizure.

Studies conducted by the Insurance Institute for Highway Safety have indicated that police using these sensors were able to detect more offenders compared with officers who did not use the sensors. Police without sensors detected 55 percent of drivers whose BACs were at or above 0.10 percent whereas police with sensors successfully detected 71 percent of the drivers with illegal BACs.

Underage Drinking and Driving

The legal drinking age in the United States is 21. No state law allows for underage drinking. If an underage child drinks and drives, the adult parent or guardian may be legally liable for any damage, injury, or death caused by the underage drinker. This is especially true if the adult purchased or provided the alcohol.

Although most states recognize the right of parents to serve their own underage child while in the home, they may not legally serve other children or provide alcohol to be consumed somewhere else. The consumption or possession of alcohol by the underage drinker is all the evidence needed for an adult to be criminally prosecuted or civilly sued.

Mothers Against Drunk Driving (MADD)

Mothers Against Drunk Driving (MADD) is a non-profit organization founded by a small group of California women in 1980 after a 13-year-old-girl was killed by a hit-and-run driver. The driver had been out of jail on bail for only two days for another hit-and-run drunk driving crash, and had three previous drunk driving arrests and two convictions.

MADD's stated mission is to look for effective solutions to drunk driving and underage drinking problems, and to assist victims of violent drunk driving crimes. MADD has initiated actions to bring about tougher laws against impaired driving, to provide for stiffer penalties for such crimes, and to increase public awareness on the perils of driving drunk.

Since 1980, MADD has continued to grow and pursue the efforts initiated by its founders. MADD has approximately 600 chapters nationwide. For more information, readers may contact MADD at P.O. Box 541688, Dallas, TX 75354-1688.

Drug Use

There is much less information concerning the role of drugs in motor vehicle accidents as compared with alcohol. It is established, however, that many legal and illegal drugs can impair driving ability, even in moderate concentrations, and may increase the risk of accidents. However, there is presently insufficient scientific evidence concerning the effect of drugs, other than alcohol, on driving.

According to a 1988 NHTSA report, the drugs with the most potential to be serious highway safety hazards are tranquilizers, sedatives and hypnotics. However, it is difficult to ascertain what contribution drugs have made in motor vehicle crashes. Information on a driver's drug use typically comes from hospital tests performed on people who are killed in crashes or hospitalized with crash injuries.

A 1992 federal study revealed that eighteen percent of fatally injured drivers have other drugs in their systems but that these drugs are most often combined with alcohol. Alcohol was found in fifty-two percent of 1,882 fatally injured drivers. Forty-three percent had blood alcohol concentrations of 0.10 percent or more. Only six percent had drugs without alcohol, and researchers found no evidence that drivers with drugs but no alcohol are more likely to be responsible for their crashes, compared with drug-free drivers. The researchers did find that drugs were related to crash responsibility when combined with alcohol, or when two or more drugs were found.

Nevertheless, the use of stimulants by tractor-trailer drivers has become a noteworthy problem. A National Transportation Safety Board investigation of fatal truck crashes found that stimulants were the most frequently identified drug class among fatally injured drivers, and were present in approximately 15 percent of those drivers.

Studies have been undertaken to assess the effect of stimulants. It has been found that occasional use of stimulants may, in the short term, enhance the performance of some tasks by increasing alertness. However, some tractor-trailer drivers may use these drugs to continue on the road for prolonged periods. Use of stimulants for this purpose is probably frequent and sustained, not occasional, and thus is potentially dangerous.

CHAPTER 4:

ACCIDENT VICTIMS AND THE CRIMINAL JUSTICE SYSTEM

In General

Victims of accidents, or their survivors, may be subjected to the criminal justice system in cases where a driver who was responsible for the crash was alleged to be criminally at fault for the accident—e.g. drunk driving—provided the criminally negligent driver survived the accident.

Few people are familiar with the workings of the criminal justice system until some type of tragedy forces them to become involved. This chapter is designed to give the accident victim or the survivors a general overview of what they may expect following an accident involving a crime.

It is against the law to kill or injure another person intentionally, maliciously, with criminal negligence, or while operating a vehicle under the influence of alcohol or other drugs. Thus, the State is responsible for prosecuting offenders who violate the law.

Unlike a civil case, there are no private "plaintiffs" in a criminal action. It is the government, on behalf of the people, who seeks the conviction. Thus, the docket generally describes the case as "The People vs. John Doe" or "The State vs. John Doe." The victim or the survivors have very little direct involvement in the prosecution, unless they witnessed the incident.

The Accident Report

The accident report is prepared by the law enforcement agency which investigates the crash, e.g., the state or local police depending on where the accident occurred. A copy may be obtained by calling the law enforcement agency handling the investigation. In order to locate the report, they will require identifying information, such as the date, time and location of the accident. If an accident number was assigned at the scene, this will usually speed up the process. There is usually a small fee for a copy of the report.

The accident report should be reviewed for accuracy. If there are any errors in the report, they should be brought to the attention of the investigating officer. If the offender was drinking, the report may indicate his or her blood-alcohol concentration (BAC) level. The offender's BAC is generally ascertained by the performance of tests—e.g., blood, urine or breath—shortly after the accident. Obtaining the offender's BAC is crucial if drunk driving was a factor in the accident.

The Law Enforcement Agency

The law enforcement agency is responsible for investigating the circumstances surrounding the accident, and obtaining evidence to support the charges. If the victim recalls any facts or witnesses not already disclosed, it is important to report this information to the investigating officer as soon as possible.

The Prosecution

Once the investigation is completed, the case will generally be reviewed by the prosecutor. After reviewing the file, the prosecutor makes the decision whether to charge the offender and, if so, what charges to bring, based on the evidence. If the prosecutor does not believe there is sufficient evidence to convict, the case may be dismissed. The standard of proof necessary to convict in a criminal case is "beyond a reasonable doubt," a very high standard of proof.

The victim or the survivors should request that the prosecutor keep them informed at all stages of the criminal proceedings. They should also request other relevant information, such as the charges that are being brought against the offender, the issue of bail, and the possibility of plea bargaining, etc.

Preliminary Hearing

In general, a preliminary hearing will be held to determine whether the prosecutor's evidence is sufficient to bring the offender to trial. The judge will make that decision unless the case is brought before a grand jury, in which case a panel of citizens makes that determination. Grand jury proceedings are closed to the public. If the grand jury decides there is sufficient evidence, they will hand down an "indictment" and the offender will be arraigned.

Arraignment

At arraignment, the offender appears in court and is informed of his or her constitutional rights, and the charges being brought. An attorney may be appointed to represent the offender, if one has not already been hired. The offender may enter a plea of guilty or not guilty at the arraignment.

If bail was not set following the arrest, it may be set at arraignment. Bail is an amount of money paid to the court to obtain the offender's release, and to ensure that he or she returns to court for further proceedings.

Following the arraignment, the prosecution and defense gather evidence in support of their respective positions. The prosecutor must be able to prove the elements which support the charges in order to get a conviction. During this time, there may be a number of pretrial hearings at which time the attorneys will advise the court of the status of the case. The victim or survivors have the right to attend all pretrial hearings, which are open to the public. Often, the defense attorney will ask for continuances—i.e., postponements—as a tactic to drag the case out until the witnesses either disappear or become forgetful. Thus, the prosecution should be encouraged to oppose defense stall tactics.

Plea Bargaining

It is common for the prosecution and defense to plea bargain a case—i.e., the defendant agrees to plead guilty to a lesser charge—to avoid the time and expense of a trial. Although the victim or the survivors may be opposed to such a practice, it would be a practical impossibility to bring every defendant to trial. If so, the criminal justice system would come to a complete halt. Thus, the court is generally in favor of plea agreements. In addition, if the prosecution's case is weak, a plea bargain will at least obtain a conviction whereas a trial may result in an acquittal.

The Trial

If the offender maintains his or her not guilty plea, the case will eventually be set down for trial. The case may be heard before the judge or a jury, depending on the defendant's wishes. It is important for the victim or the survivors to be present during the trial, to reinforce that they are real people who were injured by the defendant's actions. Nevertheless, one should be prepared for what could be extremely upsetting evidence and testimony, particularly in the case of survivors of a deceased loved one.

The trial will generally begin by opening statements made by the prosecutor and defense attorney. The prosecution then puts on their case. They call their witnesses and present their evidence. When the prosecutor questions the witnesses he or she produces, this is called "direct examination." The defense attorney is entitled to immediately thereafter pose questions of the witness. This is known as "cross-examination." After the state has presented its case, the defense will produce their witnesses and evidence in the same manner. In a criminal case, a defendant cannot be compelled to testify, although he or she has the right to do so.

After both sides have presented their case, any additional witnesses may be called to rebut previous testimony. These are known as "rebuttal witnesses." The prosecution and defense then make their closing arguments.

If the trial is before a jury, the judge will give the jury instructions concerning the proof necessary to convict the defendant. If it is a bench trial, the judge will retire to chambers to reach a decision.

The Verdict

Once the judge or jury has deliberated and come to a decision on the matter, they will render a verdict. The defendant and attorneys are brought back into the courtroom to hear the verdict. It is important that the victim or survivors understand the high standard of proof necessary to convict, so that they will not be emotionally devastated if a "not guilty" verdict is rendered. Under the "beyond a reasonable doubt" standard, if any doubt based on reason exists as to any element of the offense as charged, the verdict of the judge or jury must be "not guilty." This may be particularly difficult to accept, particularly when, to a layperson, it appears that the defendant was so clearly at fault. As set forth below, the victim or survivors may bring a civil action against the defendant, in which case the standard of proof is much lower.

Sentencing

Provided the defendant is found guilty, the case will proceed to sentencing. Sentencing may occur immediately following the conviction or be scheduled for a later hearing. In some jurisdictions, the judge decides the sentence and in others, the jury does. Evidence and procedures are different during sentencing. For example, defense witnesses will be giving subjective testimony about the defendant and why they feel he should receive a particular sentence.

It is at this point that the victim or the survivors are generally permitted to make a statement, known as a "victim impact statement." The victim impact statement is a written or oral report which details the manner in which the crime affected the victim and the victim's family. In the case of a minor or incompetent victim, the statement may be offered by the parents or legal guardian of the victim.

The victim impact statement brings to the court's attention the pain and suffering caused by the defendant, which may be expected to endure long after sentencing takes place. For example, the statement may describe the physical, mental or financial harm the offender has caused the family.

The victim impact statement also gives the victim or the survivors the chance to participate more fully in the criminal justice process and the quest to bring the defendant to justice. Many states even allow the victim to recommend a sentence or offer comments on the proposed sentence.

Most states have laws which guarantee the victim or survivors the right to make a victim impact statement, and require the court to consider the statement when rendering a decision. The statement may also be contained in the defendant's presentencing report to the court, and sent to the parole board.

Appeals

Following a conviction and sentencing, the defendant has the right to appeal the case, or in some circumstances the sentence, to a higher court to consider errors in procedure or application of the law at the trial court level. At this time, the defendant may be released on an appeal bond, pending the outcome of the appeal.

Parole

Due to prison overpopulation, convicts seldom serve their entire sentence. Convicts who exhibit good behavior during their imprisonment may be eligible for early release. Whether or not the prisoner is released is generally decided by the parole board. The victim or survivors have the right to send the parole board a copy of the victim impact statement, and to otherwise provide input into this decision.

Victims' Rights Legislation

Specific legislation concerning victims' rights has been passed in all jurisdictions, and is sometimes referred to as the "Victims' Bill of Rights." Some of the most important provisions of victims' rights legislation include:

1. The right to attend the criminal proceedings, including the trial, the sentencing, and any subsequent parole hearings, and the right to be heard;

2. The right to be notified of each stage of the criminal proceedings so that the victim can participate if he or she wishes to do so.

3. The right to compensation—such as that provided by state victim compensation programs—and restitution by the offender, including the right to recover compensation derived from the criminal's exploitation of the crime;

4. The right to be informed of all available legal remedies, including the right to pursue civil action against the criminal, e.g. to recover punitive damages; and

5. The right to be protected from harassment, including security during the criminal proceedings, and relocation

It is important to keep copies of all expenses resulting from the accident, including medical and funeral expenses, lost wages, etc. If the offender is convicted, he or she may be ordered to pay restitution to the victim or survivors.

Pursuing Civil Remedies

The civil justice system, unlike the criminal justice process, does not rule on the guilt or innocence of the criminal, nor does it subject him or her to criminal penalties, such as incarceration. The goal of the civil justice system is to determine whether the criminal—referred to as the defendant—is civilly liable for the injuries caused by the crime.

If the defendant is found to be liable, he or she is generally required to pay monetary damages to the victim or the victim's survivors. In order to be held liable, the standard of proof is that the defendant be found liable by "a preponderance of the evidence." This is a much lower standard than required in a criminal case. Thus, even if the defendant is never prosecuted criminally, or is acquitted in the criminal court, the victim is still permitted to bring a civil action against the defendant.

A crime victim has the right to pursue civil remedies against a criminal for the losses and injuries sustained as a result of the crime committed. Although, as stated above, a criminal conviction is not required in order for a victim to pursue civil remedies, the fact of a conviction in criminal court can be powerful evidence of the criminal's liability in the civil action. By taking civil action, victims are able to recover monetary damages for such items as pain and suffering, medical expenses, lost wages, and property loss.

CHAPTER 5:

YOUNG DRIVERS

In General

As a group, teenage drivers are disproportionately involved in motor vehicle crashes worldwide. In 1996, 5,805 teenagers died in the United States from motor vehicle crash injuries. Such injuries are by far the leading public health problem for young people 13-19 years old. Thirty-four percent of all deaths of 16-19 year-olds from all causes are related to motor vehicles.

In addition to teenage drivers, many teenagers die as passengers in motor vehicles. Sixty-three percent of teenage passenger deaths in 1996 occurred in crashes in which another teenager was driving. Teenagers far exceed all other age groups in terms of per capita deaths as both drivers and passengers, but their passenger fatality rates are much more extreme compared with those of older drivers.

Immaturity and lack of driving experience are the main reasons. Compared with older drivers, teenagers as a group are more willing to take risks and less likely to use seat belts. They are also more likely than older drivers to underestimate the dangers associated with hazardous situations and less able to cope with such dangers. Analyses of fatal crash data indicate that teenage drivers are more likely to be at fault in their crashes.

A 1991 Highway Loss Data Institute study reports that insurance injury claim frequencies and overall collision losses for cars insured for teenagers to drive are more than double those of cars insured for use by adults only. In order to address this serious problem, a number of initiatives are being undertaken to try to reduce teenage crashes and the deaths and injuries they cause.

Beginner Drivers

Most beginner drivers are 16 years old when they qualify for a driver's license, a relatively easy undertaking for such a great responsibility. Applicants for a first driver's license in all states must meet vision, knowledge, and skills requirements. Only thirty-five states and the District of Columbia require beginner drives to obtain learner's permits before getting their driver's licenses. Only 23 of those states require the permit to be held for a minimum period, ranging from 10 days to 1 year. In most states, new permit holders may immediately apply for licenses. Once licensed, young, inexperienced and often immature drivers in most states are permitted to drive unrestricted.

Ironically, statistics have demonstrated that this age group is at the highest risk of having a serious automobile accident. In addition, the youngest drivers have the worst record in terms of passenger deaths. More teenage passenger deaths occur when a 16 year-old is driving than any other age group.

The combination of inexperience behind the wheel and immaturity has contributed to the highest percentage of crashes involving speeding and driver error for this age group, as well as the highest fatal crash rate for single vehicles and high-occupancy vehicles. In 1996, a total of 1,539 people died in crashes involving 16-year-old drivers, including 572 16-year old drivers, 498 passengers, 366 occupants of other vehicles, and 89 pedestrians.

A number of factors have been found to contribute to the high incidence of accidents involving 16-year olds, including (i) driver error; (ii) speeding (iii) failure to use seat belts; (iv) high occupancy vehicles; and (v) alcohol use.

Driver Error

The most significant factor in accidents involving 16-year olds is driver error. Eighty-two percent of 16-year-old drivers in fatal crashes during 1996 made at least one driving error that contributed to the crashes. This compares with 68 percent of drivers 17-19 years old and 52 percent of drivers 25-49 years old.

In addition, forty-one percent of the fatal crashes involving 16-year-old drivers were single vehicle accidents. The vehicle generally left the road and overturned or struck an object like a tree or pole. Among 16-year-old drivers, this is by far the most frequent type of accident. In contrast, only 27 percent of fatal crashes with 25-49 year-olds at the wheel in 1996 were single-vehicle.

Speeding

Another common problem among this age group is speeding. Police reports indicate that 36 percent of all 16-year-old drivers in fatal crashes during 1996 were reportedly speeding or, if not exceeding the limit, going too fast for road conditions. This proportion drops steadily with age—only 21 percent of drivers 25-49 years old were reportedly speeding when their fatal crashes occurred in 1996.

Failure to Use Seat Belts

Statistics have indicated that many of the 16 year-olds in fatal crashes did not use seat belts.

High Occupancy Vehicles

Sixty-three percent of teenage passenger deaths in 1996 occurred in crashes in which another teenager was driving. Fatal crashes involving drivers this age are much more likely to occur with three or more occupants in the vehicle than are crashes involving older drivers. The occupants are usually other teenagers. In 1996, 36 percent of all crashes involving 16-year-old drivers happened when there were three or more people in the vehicle.

Alcohol Use

Statistics indicate that alcohol is not a big factor in these accidents, unlike older teens. Only 15 percent of all 16-year-old drivers killed in 1996 crashes had blood alcohol concentrations above 0.10 percent. This compares with 32 percent for older teenagers, and 53 percent for drivers 25-49 years old. However, although young drivers are less likely to drink and drive, their crash rate is substantially higher when they do.

Graduated Licensing Laws

As set forth above, under most state laws, beginning teenage drivers may get very little experience before they can obtain a license that permits unrestricted driving. Training and education programs, such as high school driver education, can help teens learn driving skills, but unfortunately it has been demonstrated that they don't produce safer drivers. More often than not it is the attitude, and not the skills, of the teen driver that are the problem. Teenagers tend to think of themselves as invincible. They generally believe they "know it all" and resist adult standards and regulations.

The success of graduated licensing systems for teenage drivers abroad has led to the introduction of similar programs in a number of states. Florida and Michigan have enacted graduated licensing programs, and plans to introduce similar programs are underway in California, Georgia, Illinois, Louisiana, New Hampshire, and North Carolina. Surveys have demonstrated that the majority of parents are generally in favor of such programs.

Studies have indicated that the most productive policies in effect to reduce teen accidents are those that restrict teenagers' driving exposure. For example, curfews that apply to all late-night activities for 13-17 year-olds have been show to reduce crashes and crash injuries.

Graduated licensing is intended to control the progression from beginner driver to unrestricted driving, lifting restrictions one by one until a young driver "graduates" to full licensure. Restrictions typically include limits on teen passengers, and a prohibition on night driving. Graduated licensing systems may also include special sanctions to discourage moving violations, belt law violations, and alcohol violations.

During the learner's phase, driving isn't permitted unless accompanied by an adult supervisor. In the intermediate phase, licensees are allowed to drive unsupervised under some conditions but not others. For example, supervision is required when driving in the late night and early morning hours.

Night driving curfews are an important element of graduated licensing systems. Most night driving curfews in force in the United States allow exemptions for driving to work or school during the restricted hours. Graduated licensing introduces unrestricted night driving only after on-the-road experience is gained during the day.

Graduated licensing is designed to introduce beginners into the driving population in a low-risk manner, protecting both them and others they meet on the roads. Graduated licensing systems could apply to all first-time drivers, not just the youngest, as they do outside the United States. In the United States, however, young people make up the majority of beginning drivers, and graduated licensing systems now being considered in some states would focus on these drivers.

Studies indicate that parents are strongly in favor of graduated licensing. A 1994 Insurance Institute for Highway Safety survey of 1,000 parents of 17 year-olds found that 90 percent favored a minimum period of supervised driving before full licensure, 74 percent favored night driving curfews, 43 percent favored restricting teenage passengers during the first few months of driving, and 97 percent favored a zero BAC for teenagers.

Fifty-eight percent of parents said they favored a graduated licensing package including many months of supervised driving practice before licensing, a night driving curfew, and prohibitions against transporting other teenagers until a good driving record has been demonstrated for six months to a year.

Graduated licensing systems have demonstrated that they are effective in reducing the motor vehicle injury risk for young people. In the states that have elements of graduated licensing, the safety benefits are evident. Studies of night driving curfews indicate that crash reductions of 60 percent or more can be achieved during curfew hours.

The National Committee on Uniform Traffic Laws and Ordinances (NCUTLO)

The National Transportation Safety Board, National Highway Traffic Safety Administration, and Insurance Institute for Highway Safety classify the licensing systems of the 50 states and District of Columbia according to the specifications of a widely accepted model graduated licensing law developed by the National Committee on Uniform Traffic Laws and Ordinances (NCUTLO).

NCUTLO's model law specifies core provisions for graduated licensing. The core provisions of the NCUTLO model include (i) a learner's phase of at least six months, followed by (ii) an intermediate phase of at least six months, and (iii) a prohibition of unsupervised driving at night for young drivers during the intermediate phase.

The NCUTLO model requires applicants for intermediate and full licenses to have no "seat belt" or "zero tolerance" alcohol use violations, and to otherwise be conviction free during the mandatory holding periods. The model recognizes that states may define "conviction free" to include only serious violations and may suspend offenders or provide lesser penalties. In most states with graduated licensing, violations by young drivers result in license suspension or extension of the holding periods.

The NCUTLO model recommends a minimum age of 16 for a learner's permit, and prohibits unsupervised driving from 10 p.m. to 5 a.m. However, failure to include these provisions does not disqualify a state from satisfying NCUTLO's core provisions.

There are a number of provisions not included in the NCUTLO model which have been proposed by other agencies. For example, the model does not include two-stage driver education to coincide with the phases of graduated licensing, as recommended by the National Highway Traffic Safety Administration. In addition, the NCUTLO model does not impose passenger restrictions during the intermediate phase, nor does it require parents or others to certify completion of a minimum number of hours of supervised driving in the learner's phase. However, the NCUTLO model does recommend certification of supervised driving in states that do not mandate any driver education.

Underage Drinking and Driving

Although young drivers are less likely than adults to drive after drinking alcohol, their crash risks are substantially higher when they do. This is especially true at low and moderate blood alcohol concentrations (BACs) and is thought to result from teenagers' relative inexperience with both drinking and driving.

Minimum alcohol purchasing age laws have been effective in reducing alcohol-related accidents involving teenagers, and many communities are strengthening enforcement of these laws. For a long time, the legal age for purchasing alcohol was 21 years old in most of the United States. Then, in the 1960s and early 1970s, many states lowered their minimum purchasing ages to 18 or 19 years old.

According to the Insurance Institute for Highway Safety, the consequences of this action indicated an increase in the number of 15-20 year-olds involved in nighttime fatal crashes. As a result of this and other studies with similar findings, a number of states raised their minimum alcohol purchasing ages—in some states back to 21 years old and in other states to 19 or 20. Subsequent research indicated that states which raised their minimum legal alcohol purchasing age experienced a 13 percent reduction in nighttime driver fatal crash involvement involving teenagers.

In 1984, 23 states had minimum alcohol purchasing ages of 21 years old. Federal legislation was enacted to withhold highway funds from the remaining 27 states if they did not follow suit. Since July 1988, all 50 states and the District of Columbia have required alcohol purchasers to be 21 years old.

According to the National Highway Traffic Safety Administration, fatal crashes among young drivers declined dramatically as states adopted older purchasing ages, and by 1996 the statistic had declined to 24 percent, the biggest improvement for any age group.

Forty-seven states and the District of Columbia have established very low legal BAC thresholds for teenage drivers, and license suspension or another penalty may result from violations of these reduced blood alcohol concentration levels. Early research from states where this policy has been implemented—including states where zero is the legal alcohol limit for teenagers—indicates it might reduce teenagers' nighttime fatal crashes.

Federal legislation passed in 1995 encourages states to adopt and enforce "zero tolerance" or a 0.02 percent maximum BAC to combat alcohol-impaired driving among drivers younger than 21 years old. All but the Mississippi and Wisconsin laws apply to drivers younger than 21, and impose a BAC threshold of 0.02 or less. Mississippi's threshold is 0.08, and the Wisconsin law applies to drivers younger than 19. States failing to comply with federal requirements by October 1998 will lose federal highway funds.

A table of state laws and restrictions concerning young drivers is set forth at Appendix 5.

CHAPTER 6:

THE NATIONAL DRIVER REGISTER

In General

The National Driver Register (NDR), is a computerized database of information about drivers who have had their licenses revoked or suspended, or who have been convicted of serious traffic violations such as driving while impaired by alcohol or drugs.

State motor vehicle agencies provide the NDR with the names of individuals who have lost their driving privilege, or who have been convicted of a serious traffic violation. When a person applies for a driver's license the state checks to see if the name is in the NDR files. If a person has been reported to the NDR as a problem driver, the license will be denied.

A directory of state motor vehicle departments is set forth at Appendix 6.

Authorized Recipients

The following individuals are legally authorized to receive information from the NDR:

1. Any individual under the provisions of the Privacy Act;
2. State and federal driver's license officials;
3. Current or prospective employers of motor vehicle operators;
4. Air carriers for pilot applicants;
5. The Federal Railroad Administration and employers of railroad engineers;
6. The Federal Aviation Administration for airmen medical certification;
7. The U.S. Coast Guard for merchant mariner certification; and
8. The National Transportation Safety Board and the Federal Highway Administration for accident investigations.

Individual's Right of Access to Information

An individual is entitled, under the provisions of the Privacy Act, to request a file search to see if he or she has a file with the NDR. In order to access this information, the individual must fill out an *Individual Request Form* and mail it or take it to their local motor vehicle agency. For a small fee, they will forward the request to the NDR.

A copy of the Individual NDR File Request Form is set forth at Appendix 7.

Employer Inquiries

An employer who employs motor vehicle operators may wish to request an NDR file check on current or prospective employees as part of their safety program provided the employee is seeking employment, or is already employed, as a driver.

In order to obtain this information, the employee may go to the local motor vehicle agency and ask for an NDR file check. For this purpose, a *Current or Prospective Employee Form* must be completed by the employee and submitted to the state in which the employee is licensed. Any information sent to the employer from the NDR should also be given to the employee.

If the employee does have an NDR file, the NDR will provide the employer with the name of the state, and the address and telephone number of the employee, in order to verify that it is the same individual. Any information on the NDR file that was reported by the states during the past 3-years will be disclosed.

A copy of the Employee NDR File Request Form is set forth at Appendix 8.

For more information on the National Driver Register, contact: Highway Safety Programs, National Driver Register 400 7th Street SW., Washington, DC 20590-0001. Tel: (202) 366-4800/Internet Address:
http://www.nhtsa.dot.gov/people/perform/driver/

CHAPTER 7:

SEAT BELTS AND CHILD RESTRAINT LAWS

Seat Belts

Manufacturers have been required to install seat belts in all passenger cars since 1968. However, it has been recognized that mere installation does not save lives or prevent injuries. Thus, states have attempted to enforce the use of seat belts. Currently, 49 states, the District of Columbia and Puerto Rico have enacted seat belt laws. New Hampshire is the only state which does not have a mandatory seat belt law. The national use rate was only 15% before the first belt law was passed in 1984, which figure has since increased to approximately 68%.

Statistics have demonstrated that the use of seat belts dramatically reduces the deaths and injuries resulting from automobile accidents. According to the National Highway Transportation and Safety Administration (NHTSA), between 1982 through 1994, safety belts saved an estimated 65,290 lives. It is estimated that, in 1994, if every front seat occupant had buckled up, an additional 9,500 deaths and about 200,000 injuries could have been prevented, for an economic savings of nearly $20 billion.

While 24.8% of the restrained occupants in passenger cars involved in fatal crashes suffered no reported injuries, only 6.3% of the unrestrained were not injured. Average inpatient care for a driver admitted into an inpatient facility as a result of motor vehicle injury is 55 percent higher if that person was unbelted. Numerous research studies also indicate that when lap and shoulder safety belts are used, the risk of fatal or serious injury is reduced by a factor of 40 to 55 percent.

The Federal Government has demonstrated its support of seat belt laws. On December 28, 1996, in his weekly radio address, President Clinton asked all Americans to always wear seat belts as the first line of defense against injuries and fatalities. On April 16, 1997, Transportation Secretary Rodney E. Slater submitted "The Presidential Initiative to Increase Seat Belt Use Nationwide."

The Initiative emphasizes the need for strong enforcement of occupant protection laws, and calls on Congress, federal agencies, governors, mayors, law enforcement, business and others to play active roles in this national endeavor.

Covered Persons

In most states, seat belt laws cover front-seat occupants only. The seat belt laws in the following twelve jurisdictions also cover rear seat occupants: Alaska, California, District of Columbia, Kentucky, Maine, Massachusetts, Montana, Nevada, Oregon, Rhode Island, Vermont, and Washington. Seat belt laws generally cover occupants of passenger cars, pickup trucks, utility vehicles, and vans, although several jurisdictions exempt occupants of some kinds of vehicles.

Standard Laws

In fourteen jurisdictions, seat belt laws are considered *standard* or *primary*—i.e., police have the authority to stop vehicles solely in connection with the seat belt violation. Those jurisdictions are: California, Connecticut, District of Columbia, Georgia, Hawaii, Iowa, Louisiana, Maryland, New Mexico, New York, North Carolina, Oklahoma, Oregon, and Texas. Police authority to enforce seat belt laws in other jurisdictions is limited, and police officers must have some other reason to stop a vehicle before issuing a seat belt ticket.

The Seat Belt Defense

Seventeen states have what is known as a "seat belt defense." This defense provides that damages collected by someone involved in a crash may be reduced if the person failed to use a belt. The reduction is permitted only for injuries caused by nonuse of belts, and, in some states, the reduction may not exceed a fixed percentage of the damages. The states which have seat belt defense laws include: Alaska, Arizona, California, Colorado, Florida, Iowa, Kentucky, Michigan, Missouri, Nebraska, New Jersey, New York, North Dakota, Ohio, Oregon, West Virginia, and Wisconsin.

Child Restraint Laws

All 50 states and the District of Columbia have child restraint laws. These laws are considered standard in all jurisdictions. Child restraint laws require children to travel in approved child restraint devices. Older children may be permitted to use adult seat belts. The age at which seat belts can be used instead of child restraints differs among the states.

It is estimated that three million child seats are sold annually in the United States. Nevertheless, according to the National Highway Traffic Safety Administration (NHTSA), almost 3000 children under age 15 are killed every year in traffic crashes. Forty percent of the vehicle occupants under age five are improperly restrained in child safety seats while approximately 90 percent of all child restraints are installed incorrectly.

Although child safety restraints have improved, and government regulations have been strengthened over the past 20 years, defective restraints, incomplete or confusing warning labels and inconsistency in vehicle and seat designs still results in child injuries and deaths. Manufacturer recalls and standardized design specifications have largely been forced by legislation.

Programs have been developed to inform parents on the proper installation of child restraints. In addition, restraints are becoming easier to use and safer, in large part because manufacturers have been found liable for inadequate warnings, and poorly worded installation instructions leading to improper installation. According to the NHTSA, improper installation is responsible for nearly 200 deaths annually. Information regarding the installation of child safety seats may be obtained from the manufacturer, the vehicle manufacturer, or the NHTSA.

The child restraint industry has been aware that many seat systems performed poorly in crash tests. The tests showed only 5 of 100 child restraint devices to be acceptable, and only one device was rated as "good". The ineffectiveness of these restraints, coupled with the number of children killed annually in car accidents, resulted in NHTSA creating Federal Motor Vehicle Safety Standard 213, which established a standardized test for child restraint systems. It requires manufacturers to test the performance of seats under the stress of a 1,000 pound pull and to determine the movement of a child crash test dummy in a 30 mph sled test.

Nevertheless, the testing has limited applicability because it does not examine the durability of restraints for children under 50 pounds in frontal crashes in bucket seats of small cars, and also fails to consider how the restraints perform in other types of collisions, e.g., rear-impact, rollover and side-impact.

Despite the changes in legislation, education, and technology, there are still some safety issues. For example, many child restraints cannot be fitted properly in smaller cars. Small cars with incompatible restraints may allow a child's head to collide with the seat back in front of the child, even in low speed collisions.

Webbing failure is another important aspect. According to the Federal Motor Vehicle Safety Standards, webbing on car seats must be at least 1.5 inches wide. Webbing narrower than this is subject to "roping"—i.e., the webbing curls or folds over itself. When this happens, the webbing cannot properly restrain the child.

Types of Child Restraints

There are five basic types of child restraints: (i) infant restraints, (ii) convertibles, (iii) forward-facing restraints, (iv) booster seats and (v) built-in child safety seats.

Infant Restraints

Infant seats are designed for babies under one year old or that weigh less than 20 pounds. The seats are rear-facing primarily to protect an infant from neurological damage during a frontal collision.

Convertible Restraints

Convertible Restraints are for infants weighing between 7 and 40 pounds. They can be placed in a rear facing position for infants weighing between 7 and 20 pounds, or in a forward facing position for toddlers weighing 20 to 40 pounds. Nevertheless, these restraints can pose a danger to small infants because they are not designed to hold the smaller infant's body securely. The five point harness has been developed to address this problem.

Forward Facing Seats

Forward facing toddler seats are recommended for children over the age of one who weigh between 20 to 45 pounds. Children under one year old or 20 pounds should not be placed in a forward facing seat because their neck is still relatively weak. If there is a collision, the child's head could snap forward sharply upon impact, causing spinal cord injury.

Booster Seat

The booster seat is designed for children weighing 35 to 60 pounds. The more recent versions which use adult seat belts are safe for children who have outgrown the other restraints.

Built-in Child Safety Seats

Built-in child safety seats are a common feature in mini-vans. They are integral seats that fold down to form child seats with harnesses, and are popular due to their convenience.

A Chart of the NHTSA Recommendations on Child Safety Restraints is set forth at Appendix 9.

Child Safety Restraints and Air Bags

Although many parents know that passenger airbags and rear-facing child restraints do not mix, some continue to place their children up front. Airbags, designed to protect an adult in a crash, deploy at a rate of 200 miles an hour. Federal and auto officials suspected as early as 1969 that air bags could injure or kill small children. In 1984, NHTSA looked into concerns that children four and under might be vulnerable to injuries from air bags. They have concluded that the rear seat is still the safest place for children.

Nevertheless, as set forth below, individuals who must transport infants and small children in the front passenger seat of a vehicle equipped with air bags may request NHTSA permission to install an air bag on-off switch. NHTSA has also considered implementing several types of "smart" air bags which would detect, by a weight or proximity sensor, whether a child is present and deactivate the air bag automatically. The technology has been available for some time but there is a cost factor involved.

Child Safety Restraints on School Buses

School bus transportation is one of the safest forms of transportation in the United States. The NHTSA requires all new school buses to meet safety requirements over and above those applying to other passenger vehicles. These include requirements for improved emergency exits, roof structure, seating and fuel systems, and bus body joint integrity. These requirements help ensure that school buses are extremely safe.

Every year, approximately 394,000 public school buses travel approximately 4.3 billion miles to transport 23.5 million children to and from school and school-related activities. Since 1984, on the average, 11 passengers per year have died in school bus crashes. Although tragic, the number of fatalities among school bus occupants is relatively small when compared to those in other types of motor vehicles.

School bus crash data shows that a Federal requirement for belts on buses would provide little, if any, added protection in a crash. The National Transportation Safety Board (NTSB) and the National Academy of Sciences (NAS) have come to the same conclusion. NTSB concluded in a 1987 study of school bus crashes that most fatalities and injuries were due to occupant seating positions being in direct line with the crash forces. NTSB stated that seat belts would not have prevented most of the serious injuries and fatalities occurring in school bus crashes.

In 1989, NAS completed a study of ways to improve school bus safety and concluded that the overall potential benefits of requiring seat belts on large school buses are insufficient to justify a Federal requirement for mandatory installation. NAS also stated that the funds used to purchase and maintain seat belts might better be spent on other school bus safety programs and devices that could save more lives and reduce more injuries.

School buses are heavier, experience less crash forces, and distribute crash forces differently than do passenger cars and light trucks. Because of this, the crash force experienced by the passengers of large buses is much less than that experienced by occupants of passenger cars, light trucks, or vans. Federal regulations require the installation of occupant restraints in motor vehicles based on the vehicle type and size. Because the safety record of school buses is outstanding, and because there is no compelling evidence to suggest that seat belts would provide even higher levels of occupant protection in crashes, NHTSA agrees with the NAS report that there is insufficient reason for a Federal mandate for seat belts on large school buses.

Rather than requiring seat belts, the NHTSA decided that the best way to provide crash protection to passengers is through a concept called "compartmentalization." This requires that the interior of large buses provide occupant protection so that children are protected without the need for seat belts. Occupant crash protection is provided by a protective envelope consisting of strong, closely-spaced seats that have energy-absorbing seat backs. The effectiveness of this method has been confirmed in the NTSB and NAS studies.

While no federal requirement exists for seat belts on large school buses, states and localities are free to install them if they feel it is in the best interest of safety in their area. However, the NAS report states that if seat belts are to be beneficial, states and local school districts that require seat belts on school buses must ensure not only that all school bus passengers wear the belts, but that they wear them correctly.

Nevertheless, small school buses, those with a gross vehicle weight rating under 10,000 pounds, must be equipped with lap or lap/shoulder belts at all designated seating positions. Since their sizes and weights are closer to those of passenger cars and trucks, the NHTSA believes seat belts in those vehicles are necessary to provide occupant protection.

School bus pedestrian fatalities account for the highest number of school bus related fatalities each year. There are about 31 such fatalities per year, about two-thirds of which involve the school bus itself and about one-third of which involve motorists illegally passing the stopped school bus. In its 1989 report, NAS stated that since children are at greater risk of being killed in school bus loading zones—i.e., boarding and leaving the bus—than in the bus, a larger share of the school bus safety effort should be directed to improving the safety of school bus loading zones. NHTSA agrees with NAS that states and localities should focus their efforts and funds toward improving school bus loading zones.

CHAPTER 8:

AIR BAGS

In General

Air bags are energy-absorbing buffers between people and the hard interior surfaces of vehicles. They are mounted in the steering wheel on the driver side of the car, and in the right front instrument panel on the passenger side. Air bags are designed to protect people in serious frontal crashes, which account for more than half of all occupant crash deaths. However, newer types of air bags are starting to become available to protect people in side impacts.

It is estimated that 67 million of the nearly 200 million cars on the road have driver's side air bags, and 38 million have passenger side air bags. As of August 1997, driver side air bags have been inflated in 1.5 million accidents. As of 1998, all new passenger cars must come equipped with an air bag system.

Air bags are considered a *supplemental* restraint system, designed to complement the seat belt and shoulder harness. They were not designed to replace the seat belt. In a serious frontal crash, a vehicle's occupant compartment and the people riding inside don't stop immediately. Instead they continue moving forward as the vehicle's front end crushes. During the fraction of a second this crushing occurs, air bags and lap/shoulder belts work together to protect people by allowing them to slow down with the occupant compartment.

The air bags help keep one's head and chest from hitting the steering wheel, instrument panel, or windshield. If there's hard braking or other violent maneuvers before the crash, the lap/shoulder belts also help keep people in positions where there's still space for the air bags to create energy-absorbing buffers between the people and the hard interior surfaces. Seat belts protect people in nonfrontal crashes as well as frontal ones, e.g., rollovers, rear-end collisions, side impacts and secondary impacts. In addition, they prevent people from being thrown from their vehicles.

National Highway Traffic and Safety Administration (NHTSA) statistics have demonstrated that air bag systems save hundreds of lives each year, and have significantly reduced the number and severity of injuries caused by automobile accidents. According to the NHTSA, from their introduction in the late 1980's through November 1, 1997, air bags have saved about 2,620 people. In addition, air bags are particularly effective in preventing life-threatening and debilitating head and chest injuries.

An NHTSA study of actual crashes found that the combination of seat belts and air bags is 75 percent effective in preventing serious head injuries and 66 percent effective in preventing serious chest injuries. That means 75 of every 100 people who would have suffered a serious head injury in a crash, and 66 out of 100 people who would have suffered chest injuries, were spared that fate because they wore seat belts and had air bags.

Air Bag Deployment

Air bags are designed to keep one's head, neck, and chest from slamming into the dash, steering wheel or windshield in a front-end crash. They are not designed to inflate in rear-end or rollover crashes or in most side crashes.

Most airbags are designed to inflate in crashes equivalent to hitting a solid barrier at 10-12 mph. Some vehicles—e.g., Mercedes and BMW—use different inflation thresholds depending on whether people are using their safety belts. Thresholds of 10-12 mph are used for unbelted occupants, but thresholds are higher—about 16 mph—for people with belts because they're unlikely to be injured in crashes at slower speeds.

Air bags will not activate when the threshold velocity change has not been reached. This can result in a fairly high speed side angle collision without the deployment of the air bags. However, if the deployment threshold levels were lower, air bags could inflate at inappropriate times such as very minor fender benders or when going over speed bumps.

Air Bag Components

An air bag system consists of several components. The sensors, which are usually mounted near the front, detect a collision by measuring the deceleration rate and direction. An impact with a solid barrier, between 8 and 17 miles per hour, will cause the sensors to activate the air bag system.

Once the sensors detect a strong enough collision, an electrical signal is sent to the control module, usually mounted up behind the dashboard, to start a chemical reaction that inflates the air bag with harmless nitrogen gas. The control module, basically a small computer, runs diagnostic checks and activates the air bags in case of an accident.

From the control module, the signal goes to the gas generator in the container holding the stowed air bag. The gas is generated by a hot filament running through sodium azide pellets. The filament heats the pellets to 300 degrees centigrade. The decomposing sodium azide produces a gas, mostly nitrogen gas, which inflates the air bags. Nitrogen gas is very friendly, non-flammable and non-toxic.

There is an ongoing debate about some of the gases produced by decomposing sodium azide. When dissolved in water, sodium azide produces hydrazoic acid. The vapors from this acid are almost as toxic as cyanide gas. Whether or not the air bag exhaust contains sufficient amounts of this toxic vapor to present a viable hazard to a vehicle's occupants remains questionable.

Some air bags are constructed of neoprene coated nylon cloth, which is very tough and capable of withstanding the rapidly increasing pressure generated by the expanding gas. The air bags are stowed tightly folded in a sealed compartment. The compartment cover, which has no welded seams, is opened by the expansion of the air bag. There are no mechanical devices to open the container. Inflation is required for the air bag to break open the sealed compartment.

The total time for the system to function, from the moment the sensors detect a collision to the full deployment of the air bag, is about 160 milliseconds, or less than 2/10ths of one second. This is extremely fast. When deploying, the inflation of the air bag may sound like a gun shot, very loud in tight quarters and unexpected. The entire sequence may be over before one realizes it happened. All a driver may find is the now limp and empty air bag in his lap.

An air bag has vent holes to allow the gas to escape and permit the occupant to ride down the collision. This is the action that prevents serious injuries. The driver is not suddenly stopped but his forward movement is slowed greatly through the collision before coming to a halt. For all of this to occur in the little time available, the inflation must be rapid to protect belted and unbelted occupants in high severity crashes.

Air Bag Injuries

In low severity collisions, rapid air bag deployment can result in injuries if the occupant strikes the bag in the early stages. Air bag induced injuries happen most often to people not using seat belts. They may be sitting close to the steering wheel.

The Insurance Institute for Highway Safety has reviewed cases of air bag induced injuries in accidents where it was determined the injuries were caused solely by the air bags. Of 280 occupants with 436 injuries, ninety six percent were classified as minor injuries, and the remaining four percent were classified moderate injuries, according to the Abbreviated Injury Scale (AIS). This scale is an anatomically based system that classifies injuries by body region on a six point scale according to threat to life, e.g., AIS-1 reflects minor injuries and AIS-6 injuries are usually fatal.

Some injuries can be expected from a collision even when the air bag was present and worked perfectly. An air bag does not restrain the lower torso so lower leg fractures can be found. As the air bag is coming towards the occupant at great speed, from 98 to more than 200 miles per hour, frontal blunt trauma is to be expected. Bruises to the face and chest and TMJ injuries may occur. There have been reports of injuries from the hyperextension of the neck but these have not been confirmed. Eye injuries are not frequent but there have been reported occurrences.

While nearly all air bag injuries are minor, a few have been serious. The New England Journal of Medicine reported a 22 year old woman suffered an atrial tear in a relatively minor crash. The injury is believed to have resulted from contact with the inflating air bag. The physicians reporting the case noted that in some circumstances "the velocity of the air bags may be sufficient to rupture the right atrium, since it is one of the thinnest vascular structures in the thorax." In one instance investigated by the NHTSA, the arm of an older female driver was splintered. Indications are her arm was resting across the air bag module in the steering wheel when the bag deployed.

Several hard impact injuries with the vehicle's interior have been found even when an air bag deployed properly. Investigations into these collisions determined there was more than one impact, as when a car is struck by another car and then goes off the road to strike a tree. The serious impact injuries were caused by the secondary impact, the one with the tree after the air bag had done it's job, protecting the occupant in the first impact and then deflating. Without seat belts, no protection was available for the subsequent impacts.

Proper Air Bag Safety

In order to reduce the risk of injury from an air bag, the NHTSA advises that occupants move the seat back and buckle their seat belt on every trip. The lap belt needs to fit over the hips, not the abdomen, and the shoulder belt should lie on the chest and over the shoulder. Any slack should be removed from the belt. In a crash, seat belts stretch and slow down movement toward the steering wheel or dashboard. Moving back and properly using seat belts gives the air bag a chance to inflate before the occupant moves forward in a crash far enough to contact the air bag.

In addition, since the risk zone for driver air bags is the first 2-3 inches of inflation, the driver should be placed 10 inches from the air bag to provide for a clear margin of safety. This distance is measured from the center of the steering wheel to the breastbone. The driving position can be modified in several ways to make sure there is a safe distance:

1. Move the seat to the rear as far as possible while still reaching the pedals comfortably.

2. Slightly recline the back of the seat. Although vehicle designs vary, many drivers can achieve the 10-inch distance, even with the driver seat all the way forward, simply by reclining the back of the seat.

3. If reclining the back of the seat makes it hard to see the road, raise up by using a firm, non-slippery cushion, or raise the seat if your vehicle has that feature.

4. If the steering wheel is adjustable, tilt it downward. This points the air bag toward the chest instead of the head and neck.

For maximum protection, in a variety of accident situations, the proper use of a seat belt and shoulder harness is required. The air bag systems, while they provide excellent protection in frontal impacts, are not as effective without seat belts and may be ineffective in other types of collisions.

The one factor that is common to all who died is not their height, weight, sex, or age. Rather, it is the fact that they were too close to the air bag when it started to deploy. For some, this occurred because they were sitting too close to the air bag. More often this occurred because they were not restrained by seat belts or child safety seats and were thrown forward during pre-crash braking.

The vast majority of passengers can avoid being too close and can minimize the risk of serious air bag injury by making simple changes in behavior. The NHTSA suggests the following:

1. Front seat adult passengers can sit a safe distance from their air bag. It is recommended that there be ten inches between the center of the air bag cover and the occupant's breastbone.

2. Infants and children 12 and under should sit in the back seat.

3. Always place an infant in a rear-facing infant seat in the back seat.

4. Everyone should use their seat belt.

Air Bag On-Off Switches

The limited number of people who may not be able to make the changes necessary for safe air bag use may benefit from having the opportunity to turn off their air bags when necessary by installation of an on-off switch. An on-off switch allows an air bag to be turned on and off. The on-off switch can be installed for the driver, passenger, or both. To limit misuse, a key must be used to operate the on-off switch. When the air bag is turned off, a light comes on. There is a message on or near the light saying "Driver Air Bag Off" or "Passenger Air Bag Off." The air bag will remain off until the key is used to turn it back on.

As of January 1998, new rules were put in place that permit consumers to choose to have the on-off switch installed for the air bags in their vehicle if they are, or a user of their vehicle is, in a risk group listed below.

Air Bag User Risk Groups

The NHTSA advises that installation of an on-off switch should be restricted to the following:

1. People who must transport infants riding in rear-facing infant seats in the front passenger seat;

2. People who must transport children ages 1 to 12 in the front passenger seat;

3. Drivers who cannot change their customary driving position and keep 10 inches between the center of the steering wheel and the center of their breastbone; and

4. People whose doctors say that, due to their medical condition, the air bag poses a special risk that outweighs the risk of hitting their head, neck or chest in a crash if the air bag is turned off. A national conference of physicians has determined that an air bag should be turned off if a safe sitting distance or position cannot be maintained by a driver because of scoliosis or achondroplasiaor, or by a passenger because of scoliosis or Down syndrome and atlantoaxial instability.

The reason that persons in high risk groups sustain injuries with air bags are because the air bag, to perform well, must deploy quickly and forcefully. The force is greatest in the first 2-3 inches after the air bag bursts through its cover and begins to inflate. Those 2-3 inches are the "risk zone." The force decreases as the air bag inflates farther.

Occupants who are very close to or on top of the air bag when it begins to inflate can be hit with enough force to suffer serious injury or death, whereas occupants who are able to sit 10 inches away from the air bag cover will contact the air bag only after it has completely or almost completely inflated.

As of November 1, 1997, the NHTSA has confirmed that 49 young children have died, all on the passenger side. Almost all of the 49 children who died were improperly restrained or positioned. 12 were infants under age 1 who were riding in rear-facing infant seats in front of the passenger air bag. When placed in the front seat, a rear-facing infant seat places an infant's head within a very few inches of the passenger air bag. In this position, an infant is almost certain to be injured if the air bag deploys. Thus, rear-facing infant seats must always be placed in the back seat.

The other 37 children ranged in age from 1 to 9 years; most were 7 or under. Twenty-nine of them were totally unrestrained. This includes 4 children who were sitting on the laps of other occupants. The remaining 8 children included some who were riding with their shoulder belts behind them and some who were wearing lap and shoulder belts, but who also should have been in booster seats because of their small size and weight. Booster seat use could have improved shoulder belt fit and performance. These various factors allowed the 37 children to get too close to the air bag when it began to inflate.

As of November 1, 1997, the NHTSA has confirmed that 38 adults have died—35 drivers and 3 passengers. Most of the adults who were killed by air bags were not properly restrained. Eighteen of the 35 drivers, and 2 of the 3 passengers, were totally unbelted. Two of the drivers who were belted had medical conditions which caused them to slump over the steering wheel immediately before the crash. A few of the drivers did not use their seat belts correctly and the others are believed to have been sitting too close to the steering wheel.

Obtaining NHTSA Permission for On-Off Switch

If an individual, or any user of their vehicle, is in one of the risk groups, they can apply to the NHTSA for permission to have the on-off switch installed. In order to gain permission, the individual must first certify that they have read the NHTSA brochure entitled "Air Bags & On-Off Switches, Information for an Informed Decision." A copy of the NHTSA brochure may be obtained by writing to the NHTSA at 400 Seventh Street, SW, Washington, DC 20590-1000, Attn: Air Bag Switch Request Forms; by calling the NHTSA hotline at 1-800-424-9393, or by accessing the NHTSA internet website at: http://www.insure.com/auto/airbags/brochure.html.

A copy of the NHTSA Air Bag On/Off Switch Request form is set forth at Appendix 10.

If an individual cannot certify that they, or any user of their vehicle, is in one of the risk groups, they are not eligible for an on-off switch.

New Air Bag Technology

Many manufacturers are installing *depowered* air bags beginning with their model year 1998 vehicles. They are called "depowered" because they deploy with less force than current air bags. They will reduce the risk of air bag-related injuries. However, even with depowered air bags, rear-facing child seats still should never be placed in the front seat and children are still safest in the back seat.

Manufacturers are also actively developing so-called *smart* or *advanced* air bags that may be able to tailor deployment based on crash severity, occupant size and position, or seat belt use. Rates of airbag inflation might be tailored to crash severity so inflation forces will be lower in less serious crashes than in ones at higher speeds. Even smarter airbags could recognize people's positions just before inflation and reduce the force if anyone is in a position to be harmed by the airbag. These bags should eliminate the risks produced by current air bag designs.

It is likely that vehicle manufacturers will introduce some form of advanced air bags over the next few years. Some vehicles already have sensors in specially designed restraints and passenger seats to detect rear-facing infant restraints and automatically switch off airbags on the passenger side.

Manufacturers have also begun installing side air bags in vehicles. Side air bags are smaller than frontal ones. They are designed to produce energy-absorbing buffers between people and the vehicle doors that are pushed against them in side impacts. Most side airbags are designed to protect the chest area, and are also likely to provide some head protection.

CHAPTER 9:

OTHER SAFETY DEVICES AND RELATED ISSUES

The National Highway Traffic Safety Administration

The National Highway Traffic Safety Administration (NHTSA), operating under the auspices of the Department of Transportation, was established by the Highway Safety Act of 1970, as the successor to the National Highway Safety Bureau, to carry out safety programs under the National Traffic and Motor Vehicle Safety Act of 1966 and the Highway Safety Act of 1966.

The NHTSA is responsible for reducing deaths, injuries and economic losses resulting from motor vehicle crashes. This is accomplished by setting and enforcing safety performance standards for motor vehicle equipment, and through grants to state and local governments to enable them to conduct effective local highway safety programs.

The NHTSA investigates safety defects in motor vehicles, sets and enforces fuel economy standards, helps states and local communities reduce the threat of drunk drivers, promotes the use of safety belts, child safety seats and air bags, investigates odometer fraud, establishes and enforces vehicle anti-theft regulations and provides consumer information on motor vehicle safety topics. The NHTSA also conducts research on driver behavior and traffic safety, to develop the most efficient and effective means of bringing about safety improvements. The NHTSA is instrumental in the regulation of the safety devices and issues discussed in this almanac, including those listed below.

The NHTSA also operates a toll-free Auto Safety Hotline to provide recall information, receive motor vehicle safety complaints and furnish consumers with a wide range of information on auto safety. The Hotline operates from 8 am to 10 pm Eastern Time, Monday thru Friday. A Spanish speaking operator is available from 8 am to 4 pm. The nationwide toll-free number is 800-424-9393. For the hearing impaired the TTY number is 800-424-9153 or 202-366-7800.

The NHTSA has 10 regional offices that provide numerous services to the states and other public and private sector customers, including technical assistance; promoting legislation; administering the Agency's grant programs; assisting in coalition building; and delivering training.

A Directory of NHTSA Regional Offices is set forth at Appendix 11.

AntiLock Brakes

The antilock brake system (ABS) has become very popular with the consumer. In fact, the total number of cars with antilock brakes is estimated to be about 18,000,000, and eighty percent of all 1994 model cars came equipped with antilocks.

Antilock brakes are designed to prevent vehicle wheels from locking, decrease the distance required to stop, and improve a driver's control during emergency braking on wet and slippery roads. In normal braking, a vehicle slows as its wheels are gradually brought to a stop. Without antilock brakes, when a driver hits regular brakes hard, the wheels may lock and the vehicle may skid. Wheel lockup can result in longer stopping distances, loss of steering control and, when road friction is uneven, loss of stability if the vehicle begins to spin.

The main advantage of antilocks is that they can reduce these problems on wet and slippery roads. Antilocks shouldn't make much difference in stopping distances on dry roads, although they can enhance vehicle stability and allow drivers to maintain steering control during emergency stops when conventional brakes might allow wheel lockup and skidding.

Antilock brakes are designed to prevent this situation. Although antilocks differ among vehicles, there are some basic similarities in how they operate. Sensors near each wheel monitor rotational speed and, as the brakes are applied and the wheel slows, an electronic control unit determines when any wheel is about to lock. The control unit then signals for reduced brake pressure, just enough to allow the wheel to start rotating again, thus preventing lockup.

Nevertheless, despite impressive testing results, research has indicated that antilock brakes are surprisingly not reducing the frequency or cost of accidents. Recent studies have indicated a 0% decrease in the overall number of accidents when comparing ABS equipped cars and non-ABS equipped cars, and a 40% increase in the incidence of single vehicle run-off-the-road accidents.

In addition, according to the Highway Loss Data Institute (HLDI), there was no reduction in insurance claim frequencies or amounts for ABS equipped cars. This was also the case in areas where antilock brakes were designed to operate most efficiently, e.g. winter in the northern states under inclement weather conditions.

As a result of these studies, on February 2, 1996, the NHTSA announced it had dropped the federal motor vehicle safety standard (FMVSS) requirement for anti-lock brake systems on all new cars.

Researchers have concluded that the reason antilock brakes are not reducing automobile accidents is that the types of collisions which antilocks are designed to prevent are less common—i.e., crashes preceded by skidding or loss of control.

In addition, many drivers do not know how to use antilock brakes effectively. Unlike the traditional way of braking on slippery roads—pumping brakes to avoid a skid—antilocks require firm, continuous brake pressure in order to activate. Drivers should never pump antilock brakes since antilocks themselves pump brakes automatically, many times a second. If the driver pumps antilock brakes during a skid, their effectiveness is reduced or eliminated. When antilocks are working, the driver may feel a pulsating sensation from the brake pedal. If the antilock feature fails to activate, brakes revert to conventional operation.

However, antilock brakes have proven to be a safety advantage for big trucks. Tractor trailers have poor braking capabilities compared with cars and, on dry surfaces, take much farther to stop—47 percent according to recent testing. On wet and slippery surfaces, their performance is even worse, and they are particularly susceptible to jackknifing during heavy braking. Antilock brakes are required on new trucks in Europe and Japan, and British fleet managers have reported that jackknifing crashes have been virtually eliminated as a result.

In March 1995, the NHTSA issued a rule requiring antilock brakes for heavy trucks, tractors, trailers, and buses. All new truck tractors were required to have antilocks effective March 1, 1997. New air-braked trailers and single-unit trucks and buses were required to have antilocks effective March 1, 1998. New single-unit trucks and buses with hydraulic brakes must have antilocks after March 1, 1999.

Bumpers

Automobile bumpers are designed to protect car bodies from damage in low-speed collisions, absorbing crash energy without significant damage to the bumper itself. Low-speed crashes occur by the thousands every day on congested streets and parking lots—the kind of impacts in which effective bumpers can mean the difference between lots of costly damage and none at all. A 1991 Insurance Institute for Highway Safety study of cars brought to

16 insurance drive-in claims centers in 4 metropolitan areas found about 20 percent of all claims for auto damage involve parking lot collisions.

Bumpers generally consist of a plastic cover and underneath, a reinforcement bar made of steel, aluminum, fiberglass composite, or plastic. A bumper system should also include mechanisms that compress to absorb crash energy—polypropylene foam or plastic honeycomb, also called "eggcrate," is often used. For a bumper to be effective, there must be some distance between the reinforcement bar and the sheet metal that it should protect.

Bumpers vary a lot in terms of both components and performance. This is true among cars of similar size and type and among cars from the same automaker. Some bumper designs put more emphasis on style than protection. For example, some car designers object to bumpers projecting beyond body parts—sometimes referred to as bumper overhang. As a result, even the most minor collisions can mean expensive damage. Lights built into bumpers may be stylish, too, but they can sustain damage in low-speed crashes

Bumpers used to be stronger. The first federal standards prohibited damage to safety-related equipment in low-speed crashes. Next came a property damage standard, effective for 1979 models, that prohibited damage except to bumpers and their attachments in 5 mph flat-barrier tests. Cars made during the 1980-82 model years prohibited all but minor cosmetic damage to the bumper itself in 5 mph tests. The result was bumpers that protected cars from damage in many low-speed collisions, meaning lower and less frequent repair bills.

However, in 1982, the federal government bowed to pressure from automakers and rolled back impact test requirements from 5 to 2.5 mph for 1983 and later model cars. The 2.5 mph standard also allows unlimited damage to the bumper and attachments. The principal argument used to justify the rollback of federal requirements was that 2.5 mph bumpers would weigh less—thus reduce gas consumption—and would cost less per car. Federal bumper requirements apply only to passenger cars. There are no federal standards for vans, pickup trucks, or utility vehicles.

The federal government does not require automakers to disclose information about bumper performance. Only California, Hawaii, and New York have bumper disclosure laws. Specifics differ, but the laws are intended to help consumers consider bumper quality when choosing among car models. Auto manufacturers are challenging the New York law in court.

Daytime Running Lights

Daytime running lights (DRLs) are a crash avoidance feature new to vehicles sold in America, but they've been used effectively for years in Canada and Scandinavia. DRLs help prevent crashes by making vehicles more conspicuous. U.S. law permits but does not require DRLs, which turn on automatically when the ignition is started and are overridden when regular headlights are activated.

DRLs typically are high-beam headlamps at reduced intensity or low-beam headlamps at full or reduced power. Tail lamps and/or turn signals also may be lit. In some vehicles, turn signals alone function as DRLs, especially when the headlamps are hidden.

DRLs are a low-cost method to reduce crashes. They are especially effective in preventing daytime head-on and front-corner collisions by making it easier to detect approaching vehicles from farther away. Nearly all published reports indicate DRLs reduce multiple-vehicle daytime crashes, which account for about half of all police-reported crashes in the United States.

No state mandates DRLs, although some require drivers to operate vehicles with lights on in bad weather. In fact, it has taken some time to have DRLs in the United States because some state lighting laws inadvertently prohibited DRLs until the NHTSA agreed to permit automakers to offer them on vehicles sold in all 50 states.

Head Restraints

Historically, the focus of head restraint requirements has been the prevention of neck hyperextension which causes the condition known as *whiplash.* The term *whiplash* refers to the motion of the head and neck relative to the torso, and the associated neck injuries occurring when a vehicle is struck from the rear.

Current research indicates that hyperextension may not be necessary for whiplash to occur. Low speed staged impacts have found that mild whiplash symptoms can occur without exceeding the normal range of motion. Animal research has demonstrated that rapid head/neck motion, within the normal range, causes spinal canal pressures to damage nerve ganglia. Further studies have shown that impacts at 44 miles per hour can be sustained without injury if no relative motion occurs between the head and torso.

Whiplash symptoms include pain in the head, neck, shoulders, and arms, and may be associated with damage to muscles, ligaments and vertebrae. Onset of these symptoms may be delayed. While some symptoms may only last a few hours or days, in some cases the effects of whiplash injury may last for years.

According to the NHTSA National Accident Sampling System (NASS) data, between 1988 and 1994, 742,340 victims sustained whiplash injuries annually. At the time of injury, these victims were occupants of passenger cars, light trucks, and vans. The average cost of such injuries was $6,045, excluding property damages, and the total annual cost associated with whiplash injury averaged $4.5 billion.

As a result, improving the effectiveness of head restraints is an area of much concern, both for the safety of the occupant, and the significant cost reduction that would result. It was concluded that head restraints were a cost effective safety device.

Since January 1, 1969 passenger cars have been required to have head restraints in the front outboard seating positions. Much of the research conducted since that time have been concerned with making the head restraints more effective.

The current Federal Motor Vehicle Safety Standards require that the head restraint must be at least 27.5 inches above the seating reference point in its highest position, and not deflect more than 4 inches under a 120 pound load. Optionally, the head restraint must not allow the relative angle of the head and torso of a 95th percentile dummy to exceed 45 degrees when exposed to an 8g acceleration. These standards were extended to light trucks and vans under 10,000 pounds on September 1, 1991.

Several computer modeling studies have shown that seat design features, other than the head restraints, also affect the likelihood of neck injury. For example, impact simulations showed that increasing recliner stiffness is likely to reduce whiplash injury and occupant rebound velocity can be controlled by the extent of plastic deformation in the seat recliner. At low speed impacts, it was found that a stiffer seat, in combination with modification to upholstery, reduced head/torso displacement and the attendant injuries.

Helmet Use Laws

Before 1967, only three states had motorcycle helmet use laws. The federal government in 1967 began requiring states to enact motorcycle helmet use laws in order to qualify for certain federal safety program and highway construction funds. Thirty-seven states enacted helmet use laws between 1967 and 1969. By 1975, all but three states mandated helmets for all motorcyclists.

As the Department of Transportation in 1976 moved to assess financial penalties on states without helmet laws, Congress responded to state pressure by revoking the department's authority to assess penalties for noncompliance. Between 1976 and 1978, 19 states weakened their helmet use laws to apply only to young riders, usually younger than age 18. Seven states repealed helmet use requirements for all motorcyclists.

In the 1980s and early 1990s, several states reinstated laws applying to all riders. Congress in the 1991 Intermodal Surface Transportation Efficiency Act created incentives for states to enact helmet use and safety belt use laws. States with both laws were eligible for special safety grants, but states without them by October 1993 had up to 3 percent of their federal highway allotment redirected to highway safety programs.

Four years after establishing the incentives, Congress again reversed itself. In the fall of 1995, Congress lifted federal sanctions against states without helmet use laws, paving the way for state legislatures to repeal helmet laws. In 1997, helmet laws in Texas and Arkansas were weakened to only apply to younger riders.

Presently, all but three states have some type of helmet use law for motorcyclists. Twenty-three states and the District of Columbia have helmet laws covering all riders, and twenty-four states have laws covering some riders, usually those younger than 18. Colorado, Illinois and Iowa are the only states which do not have any type of helmet law.

Studies indicate that only about 50 percent of motorcyclists wear helmets in jurisdictions which do not have a helmet law. However, that figure rises to almost 100 percent when a law requiring all motorcyclists to wear helmets is implemented.

In addition to motorcycles, approximately 15 states have bicycle helmet laws, generally applicable to young riders.

A table of state helmet laws is set forth at Appendix 12.

Safety Advantages

Research has demonstrated that helmet use decreases the severity of injury, the likelihood of death, and the overall cost of medical care. They're designed to cushion and protect riders' heads from the impact of a crash. Just like safety belts in cars, helmets can't provide total protection against head injury or death, but they do reduce the incidence of both.

According to the NHTSA, helmets reduce the risk of death in a motorcycle crash by about one-third overall, and the risk of fatal head injury by 40 percent. Helmets are even more effective in preventing brain injuries, which often require extensive treatment and may result in lifelong disability. Studies show unhelmeted motorcyclists are three times more likely to suffer traumatic brain injuries in a crash than helmeted riders. In the states that either reinstated or enacted a motorcycle helmet law in the past decade, helmet use has dramatically increased, and motorcyclist deaths and injuries have decreased.

Unhelmeted riders have higher health care costs as a result of their crash injuries, and many lack health insurance. Results of NHTSA's Crash Outcome Data Evaluation System study released in February 1996 show average inpatient hospital charges for unhelmeted motorcycle crash victims were 8 percent higher than for helmeted riders—$15,578 compared with $14,377.

There's no evidence that restricted helmet use laws—i.e., those that apply only to young riders—reduce deaths and injuries. In states that mandate helmet use for riders younger than 18, 3 percent of motorcyclists killed in crashes in 1994 were under 18, the same percentage killed in states without helmet laws. Helmet use rates for all riders remain low in states where restricted laws are in effect, and death rates from head injuries are twice as high in states with weak or no helmet laws, compared with rates in states with helmet laws applying to all riders.

Constitutional Issues

Courts have repeatedly upheld motorcycle helmet use laws under the U.S. Constitution. In 1972 a federal court in Massachusetts told a cyclist who objected to the law: "The public has an interest in minimizing the resources directly involved. From the moment of injury, society picks the person up off the highway; delivers him to a municipal hospital and municipal doctors; provides him with unemployment compensation if, after recovery, he cannot replace his lost job; and, if the injury causes permanent disability, may assume responsibility for his and his family's subsistence. We do not understand a state of mind that permits plaintiff to think that only he himself is concerned." This decision was affirmed by the U.S. Supreme Court.

International Helmet Laws

Laws requiring motorcyclists to wear helmets are in effect in most countries outside the United States. Among them are Australia, Belgium, Canada, Czech Republic, Denmark, Finland, France, Germany, Hungary, India, Indonesia, Ireland, Italy, Japan, Luxembourg, Malaysia, Netherlands, New Zealand, Norway, Portugal, Singapore, South Africa, Spain, Sweden, Switzerland, Thailand, and the United Kingdom. Victoria, Australia had the first motorcycle helmet use law in the world. It took effect January 1, 1961.

Cellular Phone Use and Traffic Safety

The use of cellular telephones has become commonplace in the automobile. The number of cellular phones has risen from 345,000 in 1985 to 50 million today and is expected to more than double by the year 2000. The reduced price and size of such devices has enable drivers to use driving time to get additional work done. In addition, many have purchased cellular telephones because of the convenience and security they afford in case their vehicle breaks down, particularly in an unfamiliar area.

Although cellular telephone use is a significant advance in communication, it has its drawbacks. According to a recent NHTSA report entitled *An Investigation of the Safety Implications of Wireless Communications in Vehicles*, distraction caused by cellular telephone use while driving has significantly increased the risk of automobile accidents.

The study does point out the benefits of cellular technology, such as the ability to get roadside assistance without abandoning the vehicle; and to advise law enforcement authorities about accidents, traffic problems or problem drivers, such as drunk or aggressive drivers. However, the NHTSA points out that driver inattention is known to be a primary or contributing factor in as many as 50 percent of all crashes.

The NHTSA is actively monitoring the causal connection between automobile accidents and the use of cellular telephones and other wireless communication devices, such as portable facsimile machines. The risks, benefits and recommendations discussed in the NHTSA report are set forth below.

Scope of Report

The issues discussed in the NHTSA report relate to all forms of wireless communications technology that may be used by drivers. In addition to cellular telephones, technology has introduced portable computers and facsimile machines, and a host of other palm-size devices that allow activities such as internet access; e-mail; stock exchange information, etc.

The extensive growth of such wireless communication devices over the past ten years has caused growing concern for the potential hazards of drivers using such devices in moving vehicles. Therefore, a number of legislative initiatives have been undertaken in the states to address the use of wireless communications in vehicles.

In an effort to assist these endeavors, the NHTSA has undertaken extensive research on these issues to make sure that the public, the wireless industry, and the states have sufficient knowledge upon which to make informed decisions regarding the issues and to identify needed initiatives and research to help ensure that the economic, safety, and convenience benefits of mobile wireless communications can be maintained within an acceptable margin of safety.

The NHTSA report examines the issues by reviewing available data and information on user characteristics, examining crash statistics, performing statistical analyses, and conducting a comprehensive critical review of relevant published research studies.

Legislative Initiatives

Concern over the risks of cellular telephone use in moving vehicles has prompted legislative action within the international community, as well as within some of the states. Within the international community, legislative action has, in fact, been successfully adopted, typically allowing the exclusive use of hands-free, wireless telephones while driving.

In the United States, no such attempts have been successful. However, in Washington, the motor vehicle code was amended to allow use of an "approved" headphone in association with "hands-free" wireless communications systems.

Legislative proposals have been introduced in some states that prohibit the use of cellular telephones that require the driver to manually operate or hold the phone. These legislative initiatives seem to be based on the assumption that hands-free cellular telephones are acceptable while driving in that they reduce the demands on the driver associated with dialing, holding, reaching for or picking up a handset. However, the report points out that hands-free designs will do nothing to mitigate the distraction potential of cellular telephone conversation.

The NHTSA is concerned that such legislation may inadvertently promote greater use of cellular telephones among drivers who currently limit or altogether avoid cellular telephone use while driving by implying that hands-free designs must be safe, thus increasing exposure to other potential risks that may still exist.

User Demographics

Cellular telephone use crosses all age and gender boundaries. Currently about 9 percent of the more than 50 million cellular telephones in use in the

U.S. are owned by people less than 24 years old. Because cellular telephones have become more affordable to the general population, the user profile has expanded beyond the middle-aged businessman to the young and elderly who often make personal calls. In fact, since 1990, the usage patterns have shifted from primarily business use to an emphasis on personal use.

Emergency Response Problems

According to the NHTSA report, cellular telephone users in California made approximately 29,000 emergency calls in 1985 and, in 1996, it was estimated that 2.8 million emergency calls were made. The industry estimates that 18 million such calls will be made nationwide. This has created a problem in that emergency response networks have been overburdened by multiple notifications for non-life threatening events.

In some states, including California, Colorado, Maryland, Virginia, Delaware, Texas and Florida, the cellular emergency calls are directed to the state police. The increase in the number of calls has been so great, that these states are attempting to build infrastructures to handle the volume of calls received. Although the state police surveyed are generally appreciative of the quick notification capabilities afforded by cellular telephones, when the lines are overburdened by multiple reports of the same problem, this prevents other emergencies from being reported.

Another problem exists because cellular calls cannot be traced back easily to specific locations. This presents a challenge for emergency responders to locate callers who may be disabled or unsure of their location.

Cellular Telephones and the Increased Risk of Automobile Crashes

Based on their research, the NHTSA has concluded that the inattention and distraction created by the use of a cellular telephone while driving is similar to that associated with other distractions in increasing crash risk. To identify emerging safety problems, the NHTSA primarily uses the Fatal Analysis Reporting System (FARS) and the National Automotive Sampling System (NASS) funded by NHTSA, and police crash reports collected by the states.

The FARS and NASS data sets rely upon police crash reports as a source for information regarding crashes. The FARS adds additional official records to their files, such as driver records and available medical data. The NASS program employs trained investigators to document and photograph vehicle damage and scene data, as well as to gather additional information from interviews and medical records to enhance the data file.

In recent years, both NASS and FARS have attempted to identify cellular telephone use as a pre-crash factor from police crash report narratives, although under-reporting of this factor makes an accurate assessment of the problem difficult. Nevertheless, there are trends which show that cellular telephone use is a growing factor in crashes. Driver inattention is the most frequently cited pre-crash condition for drivers who use cellular telephones.

Specific aspects of cellular telephone use have been identified which demonstrate that phone conversation rather than dialing is the most frequently reported related factor. Contrary to expectations, the majority of drivers were talking on their telephones rather than dialing at the time of the crash. A few drivers also were startled when their cellular telephones rang and, as they reached for their phones, they ran off the road. Other driver factors included driving too fast for conditions or failing to yield. The overwhelming majority of cellular telephone users were in the striking vehicle, and struck cars or other large objects that were in clear view of the driver.

On the positive side, the report has found that voice communications, if sufficiently frequent and simple to perform, appear to enhance driving performance with fatigued drivers. Simple conversations appear to have little impact on lanekeeping and speed maintenance.

The NHTSA report projects an increase in automobile crashes will accompany the expected increase in cellular telephone use unless there are certain changes in technology, and legislation aimed at reducing the risk.

Safety Enhancement Options

The NHTSA report presents a variety of options for enhancing the safe use of cellular telephones by drivers, including educational, research, enforcement and legislative considerations and initiatives.

The cellular industry itself has specifically focused on safe driving as an important consideration relating to cellular telephone use. Manufacturers of cellular products recognize the potential risks of in-vehicle cellular telephone use and make a major effort to educate their users on safety issues. For example, they encourage the use of hands-free equipment in motor vehicles, along with use of memory-dial capabilities and voice activation features.

NHTSA Goals and Recommendations

The NHTSA does not support complete restriction of cellular telephone use in the automobile. Its goal is to make in-vehicle information systems, including wireless communication, as compatible with safe driving as the state-of-the-art allows. The NHTSA report makes a number of recommendations in this regard, including:

Improving Data Collection and Reporting

The report encourages the states to record the use of a cellular telephone during a crash as part of the normal crash investigation process. This enhanced reporting would greatly improve the ability to characterize the magnitude and nature of any traffic safety problems associated with cellular telephone use while driving.

Law enforcement officers are also encouraged to note cellular telephone use on warnings or citations for moving violations, such as speeding or reckless operation of a vehicle. This type of information might be used to characterize driver-vehicle behavior and performance that serve as "distraction indicators," which might eventually be used to develop a model that uses safety-relevant indicators to predict cellular telephone-related crash rates.

Improving Consumer Education

The report advises that educational materials should be developed and disseminated to educate the driving public on the hazards of driving while distracted during cellular telephone use. These materials would inform drivers of the subtle influences of cellular telephone use while driving, such as loss of situational awareness. They could also illustrate driving conditions where cellular telephone use is particularly ill-advised.

The report discusses providing guidance on *cellular telephone etiquette*—i.e., how to politely refuse, postpone, or abruptly halt a conversation when driving conditions demand it. In addition, the report points out essential defensive driving techniques, such as teaching drivers how to recognize signs of "attentional impairment" in other drivers.

Improved Cellular Use Research and Product Development

The report further recommends that research be conducted using the National Advanced Driving Simulator (NADS) and instrumented vehicles to better understand naturalistic driver behavior while using a cellular telephone. Insights into the circumstances of call initiation, call frequency, call length, and call content would be of great benefit to formulate more realistic test protocols for cellular telephone research and product evaluation.

It is also recommended that development of "intelligent answerphone" technology be pursued for use in the automotive context. Such a system would ideally divert, record, and interrupt messages appropriately based on sensed driving conditions.

Emergency Services Calls

As set forth above, multiple calls for the same incident can overwhelm an emergency service line and actually slow an emergency services response. To address this problem, the report recommends that appropriate federal and state agencies, representatives of wireless communications associations, and national emergency services organizations examine and evaluate potential solutions to this problem.

One suggestion is the creation of a nationwide standard emergency number for cellular telephone users. The NHTSA is currently working with government and industry groups to develop a unique nationwide cellular emergency response number. Several states have already developed specific emergency phone numbers to be used exclusively by cellular subscribers.

Inattentive Driver Legislation

Reckless driving is illegal in all states. A number of states have laws on their books that specifically prohibit careless and inattentive driving. The report encourages states to actively enforce these laws, regardless of the causes of such behavior, and advises states without inattentive driving laws to consider enacting such provisions. Further, when law enforcement officers observe reckless or inattentive driving associated with cellular telephone use, this factor should be noted on the ticket.

Further information, including the a copy of the NHTSA report may be obtained from the National Highway Traffic Safety Administration Office of Public and Consumer Affairs: Tel (202) 366-9550/Internet Address http://www.nhtsa.dot.gov.

CHAPTER 10:

THE TRANSPORTATION EQUITY ACT

In General

On June 9, 1998, the President signed into law PL 105-178, the Transportation Equity Act for the 21st Century (TEA-21) authorizing highway, highway safety, transit and other surface transportation programs for the next 6 years. This new Act combines the continuation and improvement of current programs with new initiatives to meet the challenges of improving traffic safety. Significant features of TEA-21 relating to highway and traffic safety are discussed below.

Alcohol Programs

Incentives to Prevent Operation of Motor Vehicles by Intoxicated Persons

The Act provides $500 million for incentive grants for fiscal years 1998-2003 to states that have enacted and are enforcing a law providing that any person with a blood alcohol concentration of 0.08 percent or greater while operating a motor vehicle in the state shall be deemed to have committed a per se offense of driving while intoxicated.

Grants are based on the amount a state receives under the Section 402 Highway Safety program and may be used for any project eligible for assistance under Title 23 U.S.C.

Alcohol-impaired Driving Countermeasures

The Act revises the existing Section 410 alcohol-impaired driving countermeasures incentive grant program to deter drunk driving. Under this $219.5 million, 6-year program, the Secretary of Transportation will make basic grants to states that adopt and demonstrate specific programs, such as prompt suspension of the driver's license of an alcohol-impaired driver or graduated licensing systems for new drivers (Basic Grant A); or meet performance criteria showing reductions in fatalities involving impaired drivers (Basic Grant B). States receiving basic grants may be considered for up to six types of supplemental grants. States are eligible to receive grants for each of 6 fiscal years.

Open Container and Repeat Offender Measures

The Act provides penalties for states that fail to enact laws prohibiting open alcoholic beverage containers in the passenger area of a motor vehicle and establishing minimum penalties for repeat drunk-driving offenders. Failure to enact each of the required laws will result in the transfer of a portion of the state's Federal highway construction funds to its highway safety program.

The penalty is the transfer of 1.5 percent of the state's funding for those programs for fiscal years 2001 and 2002, and 3 percent for each year thereafter. The funds transferred to the safety program may be used for alcohol-impaired driving countermeasures, or may be directed to state and local agencies for enforcement of related laws.

Seat Belt and Occupant Protection Programs

Seat Belt Incentive Grants

The Act authorizes $500 million over fiscal years 1999-2003 for a new program of incentive grants to encourage states to increase seat belt use rates. The amount of funds states receive will be based on calculations by the Secretary of the annual savings to the Federal Government in medical costs, which result from the state's improvement of its seat belt use rate. A state may use these awards for any project eligible for assistance under U.S.C. Title 23.

Occupant Protection Incentive Grants

The Act authorizes $83 million over fiscal years 1999-2003 for a new, two-part Section 405 occupant protection incentive grant program to target specific laws and programs that will help states increase seat belt and child safety seat use. Under Part one of this program, the Secretary will make grants to states that adopt or demonstrate specific programs, such as primary safety belt use laws and special traffic enforcement programs. States are eligible for each of 5 fiscal years under Part One.

Under Part two of the program, the Secretary may make grants to States that carry out specific child passenger protection and education activities. States are eligible for each of 2 fiscal years under Part Two.

State Highway Safety Data Improvement Incentive Grants

The Act provides $32 million for fiscal years 1999-2002 for a new state highway safety data improvement incentive grant program to encourage states to take effective actions to improve the timeliness, accuracy, completeness, uniformity, and accessibility of their highway safety data. States are eligible for grants each fiscal year. Under this program the Secretary will make three types of grants:

(1) First-year grants for states that either (a) have initiated specific programs such as a data coordinating committee and development of a multi-year data plan, or (b) have provided certification that they have already established specific programs such as a data coordinating committee and developed a multi-year plan.

(2) Succeeding-year grants for states that, among other requirements, submit or update a multi-year data plan that meets the requirements for a first-year grant.

(3) $25,000 grants for 1 year to states that do not meet the criteria for first-year grants.

Highway Safety Research and Development

The Act continues the Section 403 Highway Safety Research and Development Program and specifies several new categories of research under Section 403, including training in work zone safety management; measures that may deter drugged driving; and programs to train law enforcement officers on motor vehicle pursuits.

Out of the funds provided for Section 403, the Act specifies allocations for the following:

(1) Measures to deter drugged driving.

(2) Vehicle pursuit training for police.

(3) Public education on sharing the road safely with commercial motor vehicles.

(4) Safety studies on blowout resistant tires and school bus occupant safety.

National Driver Register

The National Driver Register (NDR) is reauthorized with several changes to its provisions. The Act eliminates a deficiency in the NDR statute by extending participation to Federal departments or agencies, like the State Department, that both issue motor vehicle operator's licenses and transmit reports on individuals to the NDR. The Act also reduces a burden on the states and strengthens the NDR's efficiency by allowing Federal agencies authorized to receive NDR information to make their requests to and receive information directly from the NDR, instead of through a state. The Secretary is authorized to enter into an agreement with an organization that represents the interests of the states to manage the NDR's computer timeshare and user assistance functions.

The Act directs the Secretary to:

(1) Evaluate the implementation of the NDR and the commercial driver's license information system to identify ways to improve the exchange of information about unsafe drivers and drivers with multiple licenses.

(2) Assess electronic technologies that may improve the exchange of driving records.

The National Driver Register is further discussed in Chapter 6 of this almanac.

Automobile Safety and Information

The Act reauthorizes the motor vehicle safety provisions of Chapter 301 of U.S.C. Title 49, and the information, standards, and requirements provisions of Chapters 32 (General), 323 (Consumer Information), 325 (Bumper Standards), 327 (Odometers), 329 (Automobile Fuel Economy), and 331 (Theft Prevention) of U.S.C. Title 49.

The Act adopts a number of motor vehicle safety and information provisions, including:

(1) Rulemaking directions for improving air bag crash protection systems.

(2) A restriction on the use of funds appropriated to the Secretary for the NHTSA for any activity specifically designed to urge a state or local legislator to favor or oppose the adoption of a specific legislative proposal pending before any state or local legislative body.

(3) Exemptions from the odometer requirements for classes or categories of vehicles the Secretary deems appropriate.

(4) Adjustments to the automobile domestic content labeling requirements.

APPENDICES

APPENDIX 1:

STATE AUTOMOBILE INSURANCE MINIMUM MONETARY LIABILITY CHART

STATE	AMOUNT (In Thousands of Dollars)
Alabama	20/40/10
Alaska	50/100/25
Arizona	15/30/10
Arkansas	25/50/15
California	15/30/5
Colorado	25/50/15
Connecticut	20/40/10
Delaware	15/30/10
D.C.	25/50/10
Florida	10/20/10
Georgia	15/30/10
Hawaii	35/15/10
Idaho	25/50/15
Illinois	20/40/15
Indiana	25/50/10
Iowa	20/40/15
Kansas	25/50/10
Kentucky	25/50/10
Louisiana	10/20/10
Maine	20/40/10
Maryland	20/40/10

STATE	AMOUNT (In Thousands of Dollars
Massachusetts	20/40/08
Michigan	20/40/10
Minnesota	30/60/10
Mississippi	10/20/05
Missouri	25/50/10
Montana	25/50/10
Nebraska	25/50/25
Nevada	15/30/10
New Hampshire	25/50/25
New Jersey	15/30/5
New Mexico	25/50/10
New York	25/50/10*
North Carolina	25/50/15
North Dakota	25/50/25
Ohio	12.4/25/7.5
Oklahoma	10/20/10
Oregon	25/50/10
Pennsylvania	15/30/5
Rhode Island	25/50/25
South Carolina	15/30/5
South Dakota	25/50/25
Tennessee	20/50/10
Texas	20/40/15
Utah	25/50/15
Vermont	20/40/10
Virginia	25/50/20

STATE	**AMOUNT (In Thousands of Dollars**
West Virginia	20/40/10
Wisconsin	25/50/10
Wyoming	25/50/20

Note: The first number denotes the bodily injury liability maximum for one person injured in an accident; the second number denotes the bodily injury maximum for all injuries in one accident; the third number denotes the property damage liability maximum for one accident; * liability raised to 50/100 if death occurs.

**Source*: Property and Casualty Fact Book, 1997.

APPENDIX 2:

STATE MAXIMUM POSTED SPEED LIMITS FOR PASSENGER VEHICLES

STATE	INTER-STATE	LIMITED ACCESS RURAL INTERSTATES	LIMITED ACCESS URBAN INTERSTATES	OTHER LIMITED ACCESS ROADS	OTHER ROADS
ALABAMA	70	70	70	65	65
ALASKA	70	65	55	55	55
ARIZONA	75	75	75	55	55
ARKANSAS	75	70	55	60	55
CALIFORNIA	70	70	65	70	55
COLORADO	70	75	65	65	55
CONNEC-TICUT	70	65	55	65	55
DELAWARE	60	65	55	65	55
DISTRICT OF COLUMBIA	60	n/a	55	n/a	25
FLORIDA	70	70	65	70	65
GEORGIA	70	70	65	65	65
HAWAII	70	55	50	45	45
IDAHO	70	75	65	65	65
ILLINOIS	70	65	55	65	55
INDIANA	70	65	55	65	55
IOWA	75	65	55	65	55
KANSAS	75	70	70	70	65
KENTUCKY	70	65	55	65	55
LOUISIANA	70	70	55	70	65
MAINE	70	65	55	55	55
MARYLAND	70	65	60	65	55
MASSA-CHUSETTS	65	65	65	65	55

STATE	INTER-STATE	LIMITED ACCESS RURAL INTERSTATES	LIMITED ACCESS URBAN INTERSTATES	OTHER LIMITED ACCESS ROADS	OTHER ROADS
MICHIGAN	70	70	65	70	55
MINNESOTA	65	70	65	65	55
MISSISSIPPI	70	70	70	70	65
MISSOURI	70	70	60	70	65
MONTANA	none	none	none	none	none
NEBRASKA	75	75	65	65	60
NEVADA	75	75	65	70	70
NEW HAMPHIRE	70	65	65	55	55
NEW JERSEY	70	65	55	65	55
NEW MEXICO	70	75	55	65	55
NEW YORK	55	65	65	65	55
NORTH CAROLINA	70	70	65	65	55
NORTH DAKOTA	75	70	55	65	65 (Day) 55 (Night)
OHIO	70	65	65	55	55
OKLA-HOMA	70	75	70	70	70
OREGON	75	65	55	55	55
PENNSYL-VANIA	65	65	55	65	55
RHODE ISLAND	60	65	55	55	55
SOUTH CAROLINA	70	65	65	55	55
SOUTH DAKOTA	75	75	65	65	65

STATE	INTER-STATE	LIMITED ACCESS RURAL INTERSTATES	LIMITED ACCESS URBAN INTERSTATES	OTHER LIMITED ACCESS ROADS	OTHER ROADS
TENNESSEE	75	70	65	65	55
TEXAS	70	70	70	70	70
UTAH	70	75	65	55	55
VERMONT	65	65	55	50	50
VIRGINIA	70	65	55	65	55
WASHING-TON	70	70	60	55	55
WEST VIRGINIA	70	70	55	65	65
WISCONSIN	70	65	65	65	55
WYOMING	75	75	60	65	65

Source: Insurance Institute for Highway Safety

APPENDIX 3:

MODEL DWI STATUTE - NEW YORK

Article 31. Alcohol and Drug-Related Offenses and Procedures Applicable

SECTION 1192. Operating a motor vehicle while under the influence of alcohol or drugs.

1. Driving while ability impaired. No person shall operate a motor vehicle while the person's ability to operate such motor vehicle is impaired by the consumption of alcohol.

2. Driving while intoxicated; per se. No person shall operate a motor vehicle while such person has .10 of one per centum or more by weight of alcohol in the person's blood as shown by chemical analysis of such person's blood, breath, urine or saliva, made pursuant to the provisions of section eleven hundred ninety-four of this article.

3. Driving while intoxicated. No person shall operate a motor vehicle while in an intoxicated condition.

4. Driving while ability impaired by drugs. No person shall operate a motor vehicle while the person's ability to operate such a motor vehicle is impaired by the use of a drug as defined in this chapter.

5. Commercial motor vehicles: per se - level I. Notwithstanding the provisions of section eleven hundred ninety-five of this article, no person shall operate a commercial motor vehicle while such person has .04 of one per centum or more but not more than .07 of one per centum by weight of alcohol in the person's blood as shown by chemical analysis of such person's blood, breath, urine or saliva, made pursuant to the provisions of section eleven hundred ninety-four of this article; provided, however, nothing contained in this subdivision shall prohibit the imposition of a charge of a violation of subdivision one of this section, or of section eleven hundred ninety-two-a of this article where a person under the age of twenty-one operates a commercial motor vehicle where a chemical analysis of such person's blood, breath, urine, or saliva, made pursuant to the provisions of section eleven hundred ninety-four of this article, indicates that such operator has .02 of one per centum or more but less than .04 of one per centum by weight of alcohol in such operator's blood.

6. Commercial motor vehicles; per se - level II. Notwithstanding the provisions of section eleven hundred ninety-five of this article, no person shall

operate a commercial motor vehicle while such person has more than .07 of one per centum but less than .10 of one per centum by weight of alcohol in the person's blood as shown by chemical analysis of such person's blood, breath, urine or saliva, made pursuant to the provisions of section eleven hundred ninety-four of this article; provided, however, nothing contained in this subdivision shall prohibit the imposition of a charge of a violation of subdivision one of this section.

7. Where applicable. The provisions of this section shall apply upon public highways, private roads open to motor vehicle traffic and any other parking lot. For the purposes of this section "parking lot" shall mean any area or areas of private property, including a driveway, near or contiguous to and provided in connection with premises and used as a means of access to and egress from a public highway to such premises and having a capacity for the parking of four or more motor vehicles. The provisions of this section shall not apply to any area or areas of private property comprising all or part of property on which is situated a one or two family residence.

8. Effect of prior out-of-state conviction. A prior out-of-state conviction for operating a motor vehicle while under the influence of alcohol or drugs shall be deemed to be a prior conviction of a violation of subdivision one of this section for purposes of determining penalties imposed under this section or for purposes of any administrative action required to be taken pursuant to subdivision two of section eleven hundred ninety-three of this article; provided, however, that such conduct, had it occurred in this state, would have constituted a violation of any of the provisions of this section. This subdivision shall only apply to convictions occurring on or after November twenty-ninth, nineteen hundred eighty-five.

8-a. Effect of prior finding of having consumed alcohol. A prior finding that a person under the age of twenty-one has operated a motor vehicle after having consumed alcohol pursuant to section eleven hundred ninety-four-a of this article shall have the same effect as a prior conviction of a violation of subdivision one of this section solely for the purpose of determining the length of any license suspension or revocation required to be imposed under any provision of this article, provided that the subsequent offense is committed prior to the expiration of the retention period for such prior offense or offenses set forth in paragraph (k) of subdivision one of section two hundred one of this chapter.

9. Conviction of a different charge. A driver may be convicted of a violation of subdivision one, two or three of this section, notwithstanding that the charge laid before the court alleged a violation of subdivision two or three of

this section,and regardless of whether or not such conviction is based on a plea of guilty.

SECTION 1192-a. Operating a motor vehicle after having consumed alcohol; under the age of twenty-one; per se.

No person under the age of twenty-one shall operate a motor vehicle after having consumed alcohol as defined in this section. For purposes of this section, a person under the age of twenty-one is deemed to have consumed alcohol only if such person has .02 of one per centum or more but not more than .07 of one per centum by weight of alcohol in the person's blood, as shown by chemical analysis of such person's blood, breath, urine or saliva, made pursuant to the provisions of section eleven hundred ninety-four of this article. Any person who operates a motor vehicle in violation of this section, and who is not charged with a violation of any subdivision of section eleven hundred ninety-two of this article arising out of the same incident shall be referred to the department for action in accordance with the provisions of section eleven hundred ninety-four-a of this article. Except as otherwise provided in subdivision five of section eleven hundred ninety-two of this article, this section shall not apply to a person who operates a commercial motor vehicle. Notwithstanding any provision of law to the contrary, a finding that a person under the age of twenty-one operated a motor vehicle after having consumed alcohol in violation of this section is not a judgment of conviction for a crime or any other offense.

SECTION 1193. Sanctions.

1. Criminal penalties.

(a) Driving while ability impaired. A violation of subdivision one of section eleven hundred ninety-two of this article shall be a traffic infraction and shall be punishable by a fine of not less than three hundred dollars nor more than five hundred dollars or by imprisonment in a penitentiary or county jail for not more than fifteen days, or by both such fine and imprisonment. A person who operates a vehicle in violation of such subdivision after having been convicted of a violation of any subdivision of section eleven hundred ninety-two of this article within the preceding five years shall be punished by a fine of not less than five hundred dollars nor more than seven hundred fifty dollars, or by imprisonment of not more than thirty days in a penitentiary or county jail or by both such fine and imprisonment. A person who operates a vehicle in violation of such subdivision after having been convicted two or more times of a violation of any subdivision of section eleven hundred ninety-two of this article within the preceding ten years shall be guilty of a misdemeanor, and shall be punished by a fine of not less than seven hundred fifty dollars nor more than fifteen hundred dollars, or by imprisonment of not more than one hundred eighty days in a penitentiary or county jail or by both such fine and imprisonment.

(b) Driving while intoxicated or while ability impaired by drugs; misdemeanor offenses. A violation of subdivision two, three or four of section eleven hundred ninety-two of this article shall be a misdemeanor and shall be punishable by a fine of not less than five hundred dollars nor more than one thousand dollars, or by imprisonment in a penitentiary or county jail for not more than one year, or by both such fine and imprisonment.

(c) Felony offenses.

(i) A person who operates a vehicle in violation of subdivision two, three or four of section eleven hundred ninety-two of this article after having been convicted of a violation of subdivision two, three or four of such section or of vehicular assault in the second or first degree, as defined, respectively, in sections 120.03 and 120.04 of the penal law or of vehicular manslaughter in the second or first degree, as defined, respectively, in sections 125.12 and 125.13 of such law, within the preceding ten years, shall be guilty of a class E felony, and shall be punished by a fine of not less than one thousand dollars nor more than five thousand dollars or by a period of imprisonment as provided in the penal law, or by both such fine and imprisonment.

(ii) A person who operates a vehicle in violation of subdivision two, three or four of section eleven hundred ninety-two of this article after having been convicted of a violation of subdivision two, three or four of such section or of vehicular assault in the second or first degree, as defined, respectively, in sections 120.03 and 120.04 of the penal law or of vehicular manslaughter in the second or first degree, as defined, respectively, in sections 125.12 and 125.13 of such law, twice within the preceding ten years, shall be guilty of a class D felony, and shall be punished by a fine of not less than two thousand dollars nor more than ten thousand dollars or by a period of imprisonment as provided in the penal law, or by both such fine and imprisonment.

Where the court imposes a sentence for a violation of section eleven hundred ninety-two of this article, the court may require the defendant, as a part of or as a condition of such sentence, to attend a single session conducted by a victims impact program. For purposes of this section, "victims impact program" means a program operated by a county, a city with a population of one million or more, by a not-for-profit organization authorized by any such county or city, or a combination thereof, in which presentations are made concerning the impact of operating a motor vehicle while under the influence of alcohol or drugs to one or more persons who have been convicted of such offenses. A description of any such program shall be filed with the commissioner and with the coordinator of the special traffic options program for driving while intoxicated established pursuant to section eleven hundred ninety-seven of this article, and shall be made available to the court upon request. Nothing contained herein shall be construed to require any governmental entity to create such a victim impact program.

2. License sanctions.

(a) Suspensions. Except as otherwise provided in this subdivision, a license shall be suspended and a registration may be suspended for the following periods:

(1) Driving while ability impaired. Ninety days, where the holder is convicted of a violation of subdivision one of section eleven hundred ninety-two of this article;

(2) Persons under the age of twenty-one; driving after having consumed alcohol. Six months, where the holder has been found to have operated a motor vehicle after having consumed alcohol in violation of section eleven hundred ninety-two-a of this article where such person was under the age of twenty-one at the time of commission of such violation.

(b) Revocations. A license shall be revoked and a registration may be revoked for the following minimum periods:

(1) Driving while ability impaired; prior offense. Six months, where the holder is convicted of a violation of subdivision one of section eleven hundred ninety-two of this article committed within five years of a conviction for a violation of any subdivision of section eleven hundred ninety-two of this article.

(1-a) Driving while ability impaired; misdemeanor offense. Six months, where the holder is convicted of a violation of subdivision one of section eleven hundred ninety-two of this article committed within ten years of two previous convictions for a violation of any subdivision of section eleven hundred ninety-two of this article.

(2) Driving while intoxicated or while ability impaired by drugs. Six months, where the holder is convicted of a violation of subdivision two, three or four of section eleven hundred ninety-two of this article.

(3) Driving while intoxicated or while ability impaired by drugs; prior offense. One year, where the holder is convicted of a violation of subdivision two, three or four of section eleven hundred ninety-two of this article committed within ten years of a conviction for a violation of subdivision two, three or four of section eleven hundred ninety-two of this article.

(6) Persons under the age of twenty-one. One year, where the holder is convicted of or adjudicated a youthful offender for a violation of any subdivision of section eleven hundred ninety-two of this article where such person was under the age of twenty-one at the time of commission of such violation.

(7) Persons under the age of twenty-one; prior offense or finding. One year or until the holder reaches the age of twenty-one, whichever is the greater period of time, where the holder has been found to have operated a motor vehicle after having consumed alcohol in violation of section eleven hundred ninety-two-a of this article, or is convicted of, or adjudicated a youthful offender for, a violation of any subdivision of section eleven hundred ninety-two of this article and has previously been found to have operated a motor vehicle after having consumed alcohol in violation of section eleven hundred ninety-two-a of this article, or has previously been convicted of, or adjudicated a youthful offender for, any violation of section eleven hundred ninety-two of this article not arising out of the same incident.

SECTION 1197. Special traffic options program for driving while intoxicated. [STOP-DWI]

"The program", as used in this section, shall mean the special traffic options program for driving while intoxicated, a program established pursuant to this section, and approved by the commissioner of motor vehicles.

1. Program establishment.

(a) Where a county establishes a special traffic options program for driving while intoxicated, pursuant to this section, it shall receive fines and forfeitures collected by any court, judge, magistrate or other officer within that county, including, where appropriate, a hearing officer acting on behalf of the commissioner:

3. Purposes.

(a) The program shall provide a plan for coordination of county, town, city and village efforts to reduce alcohol-related traffic injuries and fatalities.

(b) The program shall, where approved by the county board or other governing body, provide funding for such activities as the board or other body may approve, for the above-described purposes.

4. Duties of the coordinator; reports.

(a) It shall be the duty of the coordinator to:

(1) Render annually or at the request of the county legislature or other governing body of the county, a verified account of all moneys received and expended by the coordinator or under the coordinator's direction and an account of other pertinent matters.

(2) Submit annually or upon request of the chief fiscal officer of each county participating in the program, in such manner as may be required by law, an estimate of the funds required to carry out the purposes of this section.

(3) Make an annual report to the commissioner, which shall be due on or before the first day of April of each year following the implementation of said program, and shall include the following:

a. the progress, problems and other matters related to the administration of said program; and

b. an assessment of the effectiveness of the program within the geographic area of the county participating therein and any and all recommendations for expanding and improving said program.

(b) Any annual report shall also contain the following, in a form prescribed by the commissioner:

(1) Number of arrests for violations of section eleven hundred ninety-two of this article and subdivision two of section five hundred eleven of this chapter;

(2) Number and description of dispositions resulting therefrom;

(3) Number of suspensions issued in the county for alleged refusals to submit to chemical tests;

(4) Total fine moneys returned to the participating county in connection with the program;

(5) Contemplated programs;

(6) Distribution of moneys in connection with program administration;

(7) Any other information required by the commissioner.

5. Functions of the coordinator.

In addition to the duties of the coordinator as provided in subdivision four of this section, the coordinator shall perform the following functions:

(a) Formulate a special traffic options program for driving while intoxicated and coordinate efforts of interested parties and agencies engaged in alcohol traffic safety, law enforcement, adjudication, rehabilitation and preventive education.

(b) Receive proposals from county, town, city or village agencies or non-governmental groups for activities related to alcohol traffic safety and to submit them to the county board of legislators or other such governing body, together with a recommendation for funding of the activity if deemed appropriate.

(c) Cooperate with and assist local officials within the county in the formulation and execution of alcohol traffic safety programs including enforcement, adjudication, rehabilitation and education.

(d) Study alcohol traffic safety problems with the county and recommend to the appropriate legislative bodies, departments or commissions, such changes in rules, orders, regulations and existing law as the coordinator may deem advisable.

(e) Promote alcohol and drug-related traffic safety education for drivers.

(f) Obtain and assemble data on alcohol-related accident arrests, convictions and accidents and to analyze, study, and consolidate such data for educational, research and informational purposes

SECTION 1227. Consumption of alcoholic beverages in certain motor vehicles.

1. The drinking of alcoholic beverages, in a motor vehicle being driven upon the public highways is prohibited. Any operator or passenger violating this section shall be guilty of a traffic infraction. The provisions of this section shall not be deemed to prohibit the drinking of alcoholic beverages by passengers in passenger vehicles operated pursuant to a certificate or permit issued by the public service commission or interstate commerce commission.

2. For the purposes of this section, a passenger vehicle shall mean a vehicle designed to carry ten or more passengers and used to carry passengers for profit or hire.

APPENDIX 4:

STATE DUI/DWI LAWS

STATE	BAC ILLEGAL PER SE - ALL DRIVERS	BAC ILLEGAL PER SE - YOUNG DRIVERS (UNDER 21)	ADMINIS-TRATIVE LICENSE SUSPENSION - 1ST OFFENSE (BAC FOR ALL DRIVERS)	DRIVING PRIVILEGES RESTORED DURING SUSPENSION	IGNITION INTER-LOCKS	VEHCLE FOR-FEITURE	SEE FOOT-NOTE
ALABAMA	0.08	0.02	90 DAYS	NO	NO	NO	
ALASKA	0.10	0.00	90 DAYS	AFTER 30 DAYS	YES	YES	
ARIZONA	0.10	0.00	90 DAYS	AFTER 30 DAYS	NO	YES	
ARKANSAS	0.10	0.02	120 DAYS	YES	YES	YES	2
CALIFOR-NIA	0.08	0.01	4 MONTHS	AFTER 30 DAYS	YES	YES	2
COLORADO	0.10	0.02	3 MONTHS	NO	YES	NO	N/A
CONNECTI-CUT	0.10	0.02	90 DAYS	YES	NO	NO	N/A
DELAWARE	0.10	0.02	3 MONTHS	NO	YES	NO	1-3
DISTRICT OF COLUMBIA	0.10	0.02	90 DAYS	YES	NO	NO	N/A
FLORIDA	0.08	0.02	6 MONTHS	YES	YES	NO	3
GEORGIA	0.10	0.02	1 YEAR	YES	YES	YES	N/A
HAWAII	0.08	0.02	3 MONTHS	AFTER 30 DAYS	YES	NO	N/A
IDAHO	0.08	0.02	90 DAYS	AFTER 30 DAYS	YES	NO	N/A
ILLINOIS	0.08	0.00	3 MONTHS	AFTER 30 DAYS	YES	NO	N/A
INDIANA	0.10	0.02	180 DAYS	AFTER 30 DAYS	YES	NO	3
IOWA	0.10	0.02	180 DAYS	YES	YES	NO	3
KANSAS	0.08	0.02	30 DAYS	NO	YES	NO	3

STATE	BAC ILLEGAL PER SE - ALL DRIVERS	BAC ILLEGAL PER SE - YOUNG DRIVERS (UNDER 21)	ADMINIS-TRATIVE LICENSE SUSPENSION - 1ST OFFENSE (BAC FOR ALL DRIVERS)	DRIVING PRIVILEGES RESTORED DURING SUSPENSION	IGNITION INTER-LOCKS	VEHCLE FOR-FEITURE	SEE FOOT-NOTE
KENTUCKY	0.10	0.02	N/A	N/A	NO	NO	N/A
LOUISIANA	0.10	0.02	90 DAYS	AFTER 30 DAYS	YES	NO	N/A
MAINE	0.08	0.00	90 DAYS	YES	YES	NO	3
MARYLAND	0.10	0.02	45 DAYS	YES	YES	NO	3
MASSA-CHUSETTS	NONE	0.02	90 DAYS	NO	NO	NO	1
MICHIGAN	0.10	0.02	N/A	N/A	YES	NO	N/A
MINNESOTA	0.10	0.00	90 DAYS	AFTER 15 DAYS	NO	YES	3
MISSISSIPPI	0.10	0.08	90 DAYS	NO	NO	YES	N/A
MISSOURI	0.10	0.02	30 DAYS	NO	YES	YES	N/A
MONTANA	0.10	0.02	N/A	N/A	YES	YES	3
NEBRASKA	0.10	0.02	90 DAYS	AFTER 30 DAYS	YES	NO	N/A
NEVADA	0.10	0.02	90 DAYS	AFTER 45 DAYS	YES	NO	N/A
NEW HAMPSHIRE	0.08	0.02	6 MONTHS	NO	NO	NO	3
NEW JERSEY	0.10,0.01	N/A	N/A	NO	NO	N/A	
NEW MEXICO	0.08	0.02	90 DAYS	AFTER 30 DAYS	NO	NO	N/A
NEW YORK	0.10	0.02	VARIABLE	YES	YES	YES	3-4
NORTH CAROLINA	0.08	0.00	10 DAYS	NO	YES	YES	N/A
NORTH DAKOTA	0.10	0.02	91 DAYS	AFTER 30 DAYS	YES	YES	3
OHIO	0.10	0.02	90 DAYS	AFTER 15 DAYS	YES	YES	3

STATE	BAC ILLEGAL PER SE - ALL DRIVERS	BAC ILLEGAL PER SE - YOUNG DRIVERS (UNDER 21)	ADMINIS-TRATIVE LICENSE SUSPENSION - 1ST OFFENSE (BAC FOR ALL DRIVERS)	DRIVING PRIVILEGES RESTORED DURING SUSPENSION	IGNITION INTER-LOCKS	VEHCLE FOR-FEITURE	SEE FOOT-NOTE
OKLAHOMA	0.10	0.00	180 DAYS	YES	YES	NO	N/A
OREGON	0.08	0.00	90 DAYS	AFTER 30 DAYS	YES	NO	3
PENNSYL-VANIA	0.10	0.02	N/A	N/A	NO	YES	N/A
RHODE ISLAND	0.10	0.02	N/A	N/A	YES	YES	N/A
SOUTH CAROLINA	NONE	N/A	N/A	N/A	NO	YES	1
SOUTH DAKOTA	0.10	N/A	N/A	N/A	NO	NO	3
TENNESSEE	0.10	0.02	N/A	N/A	YES	YES	N/A
TEXAS	0.10	0.00	60 DAYS	YES	YES	YES	N/A
UTAH	0.08	0.00	90 DAYS	NO	YES	NO	3
VERMONT	0.08	0.02	90 DAYS	NO	NO	NO	N/A
VIRGINIA	0.08	0.02	7 DAYS	NO	YES	NO	3
WASHING-TON	0.10	0.02	N/A	N/A	YES	YES	N/A
WEST VIRGINIA	0.10	0.02	6 MONTHS	AFTER 30 DAYS	YES	NO	N/A
WISCONSIN	0.10	0.02	6 MONTHS	YES	YES	YES	N/A
WYOMING	0.10	N/A	90 DAYS	YES	NO	NO	3

Notes:

1. Laws in Massachusetts and South Carolina are not per se laws. A BAC of 0.10 percent in South Carolina and 0.08 percent in Massachusetts is evidence of alcohol impairment but isn't illegal per se. In Delaware, the 0.02 percent BAC law for young drivers isn't a per se law.

2. Drivers usually must demonstrate special hardship to justify restoring privileges during suspension, and then privileges often are restricted.

3. An offender's vehicle may be impounded or immobilized, the registration may be suspended, or the license tags may be confiscated. In New York, registration suspen-

sion applies only to offenders younger than 21. In Montana, impoundment applies only to offenders younger than 18.

4. In New York, administrative license suspension lasts until prosecution is complete.

Source: Insurance Institute for Highway Safety.

APPENDIX 5:

STATE YOUNG DRIVERS LAWS

STATE	MINIMUM AGE - LEARNER'S PERMIT (LP)	MINIMUM AGE - REGULAR LICENSE	LP REQUIRED BEFORE REGULAR LICENSE	MINIMUM LP PERIOD	LP EXPIRA-TION	NIGHT DRIVING RES-TRICTIONS	SEE FOOT-NOTE
ALABAMA	15	16	no	N/A	4 YEARS	NO	N/A
ARKANSAS	14	16	YES	30 DAYS	60 DAYS	NO	N/A
COLORADO	15-3 MOS	16	YES	90 DAYS	8 MONTHS	NO	N/A
CONEC-TICUT	16	16-6 MOS	YES	180 DAYS	UNTIL AGE 18	NO	1
DISTRICT OF COLUMBIA	16	16	YES	N/A	3 MONTHS	NO	N/A
FLORIDA	15	16	YES	180 DAYS	6 YEARS	11PM-6AM AT AGE 16; 1-5 AM AT AGE 17	N/A
HAWAII	15	15	YES	90 DAYS	180 DAYS	NO	N/A
IDAHO	15	15	NO	N/A	180 DAYS	NO	N/A
ILLINOIS	15	16	YES	90 DAYS	2 YEARS	11PM-6AM FROM MON-THURS AND MIDNIGHT TO 6AM FROM FRIDAY TO SUNDAY UNTIL AGE 17	N/A
INDIANA	15	16	YES	1 MONTH	UNTIL AGE 16-3MOS	NO	N/A

STATE	MINIMUM AGE - LEARNER'S PERMIT (LP)	MINIMUM AGE - REGULAR LICENSE	LP REQUIRED BEFORE REGULAR LICENSE	MINIMUM LP PERIOD	LP EXPIRA-TION	NIGHT DRIVING RES-TRICTIONS	SEE FOOT-NOTE
IOWA	14	16	YES	N/A	2 YEARS FROM BIRTHDAY IN YEAR OF ISSUANCE	NO	N/A
KANSAS	14	16	NO	N/A	1 YEAR	NO	N/A
KENTUCKY	16	16-6MOS	YES	180 DAYS	1 YEAR	NO	N/A
LOUISI-ANA	15	16	YES	90 DAYS	4 YEARS	11PM-5AM UNTIL AGE 17	N/A
MARYLAND	15-9MOS	16	YES	14 DAYS	180 DAYS	MIDNIGHT-5AM FOR 1 YEAR OR UNTIL AGE 18	N/A
MASSA-CHUSETTS	16	16-6MOS	YES	N/A	1 YEAR	1-4AM UNTIL AGE 18	N/A
MINNE-SOTA	15	16	YES	180 DAYS	1 YEAR	NO	N/A
MISSIS-SIPPI	15	16	YES	30 DAYS	1 YEAR	NO	N/A
MISSOURI	15-6MOS	16	NO	N/A	6 MONTHS	NO	N/A
MONTANA	14-6MOS	15	NO	N/A	6 MONTHS	NO	N/A
NEBRASKA	15	16	NO	N/A	1 YEAR	NO	N/A
NEVADA	15-6MOS	16	NO	N/A	8 MONTHS	NO	N/A
NEW HAMP-SHIRE	16	16-3MOS	YES	90 DAYS	N/A	1-5AM UNTIL AGE 18	N/A
NEW JERSEY	16	17	YES	N/A	1 YEAR-3MOS	NO	N/A
NEW MEXICO	15	15	YES	N/A	6 MONTHS	NO	N/A

STATE	MINIMUM AGE - LEARNER'S PERMIT (LP)	MINIMUM AGE - REGULAR LICENSE	LP REQUIRED BEFORE REGULAR LICENSE	MINIMUM LP PERIOD	LP EXPIRA-TION	NIGHT DRIVING RES-TRICTIONS	SEE FOOT-NOTE
NEW YORK	16	16	YES	N/A	3 YEARS	9PM-5AM UNTIL AGE 18	2
NORTH CAROLINA	15	16	YES	1 YEAR	18 MONTHS	9PM-5AM FOR 6 MONTHS OR UNTIL AGE 18	N/A
NORTH DAKOTA	14	16	YES	90 DAYS	1 YEAR	NO	N/A
OHIO	15-6MOS	16	YES	6 MONTHS	1 YEAR	1AM-5AM UNTIL AGE 17	N/A
OKLA-HOMA	15-6MOS	16	NO	N/A	4 YEARS	NO	N/A
OREGON	15	16	NO	N/A	18 MONTHS	NO	N/A
PENNSYL-VANIA	16	16	YES	N/A	120 DAYS	MIDNIGHT-5AM UNTIL AGE 18	N/A
RHODE ISLAND	16	16	YES	N/A	180 DAYS	NO	N/A
SOUTH CAROLINA	15	15	YES	15 DAYS	12 MONTHS	6PM-6AM EST AND 8PM-6AM EDT UNTIL AGE 16	N/A
SOUTH DAKOTA	14	16	NO	N/A	180 DAYS	NO	4
TEN-NESSEE	15	16	NO	90 DAYS	1 YEAR	NO	3
TEXAS	15	16	YES	N/A	1 YEAR	NO	N/A
UTAH	16	16	YES	N/A	6 MONTHS	NO	5
VERMONT	15	16	YES	N/A	2 YEARS	NO	N/A

STATE	MINIMUM AGE - LEARNER'S PERMIT (LP)	MINIMUM AGE - REGULAR LICENSE	LP REQUIRED BEFORE REGULAR LICENSE	MINIMUM LP PERIOD	LP EXPIRA-TION	NIGHT DRIVING RES-TRICTIONS	SEE FOOT-NOTE
VIRGINIA	15	16	YES	180 DAYS	IN-DEFINITE	NO	N/A
WASHING-TON	15	16	YES	N/A	1 YEAR	NO	N/A
WEST VIRGINIA	15	16	YES	N/A	UNTIL AGE 16-2MOS	NO	N/A
WIS-CONSIN	15-6MOS	16	YES	N/A	6 MONTHS	NO	N/A
WYOMING	15	16	NO	10 DAYS	1 YEAR	NO	N/A

Notes:

1. In Connecticut, the 180-day minimum learner's period is reduced to 120 days for applicants who have completed approved driver education.

2. In New York, licensing laws prohibit people with DJ licenses (16 and 17 year-olds) from driving in New York City.

3. In Tennessee, the 3-month minimum learner's period is waived for applicants who have completed approved driver education.

4. South Dakota issues a restricted license which allows 14 and 15 year-olds to drive unsupervised between the h ours of 6am to 8pm; at other times they are allowed to drive only under the supervision of a parent or guardian. The restricted license becomes a regular license when the holder turns 16.

5. In Utah, instructional permits also are issued to people 15 years and 9 months old. Valid for 1 year, these permit driving only with a professional driving instructor. Instructors may give practice permits, valid for 90 days, that allow driving only with a parent or guardian.

Source: Insurance Institute for Highway Safety

APPENDIX 6:

DIRECTORY OF STATE MOTOR VEHICLE AGENCIES

STATE	AGENCY	ADDRESS	TELEPHONE
ALABAMA	Department of Public Safety, Driver License Records Unit	P.O. Box 1471, Montgomery, AL 36192-2301	(205) 242-4400
ALASKA	Department of Public Safety, Division of Motor Vehicles Driver Services	P.O. Box 20020, Juneau, AK 99802- 0020	(907) 465-4335
ARIZONA	Motor Vehicle Division, Office of Driver Improvement	P.O. Box 2100, Phoenix, AZ 85001	(602) 255-0072
ARKANSAS	Office of Driver Services, Driver Control Section	P.O. Box 1272, Little Rock, AR 72203	(501) 682-1400
CALIFORNIA	Department of Motor Vehicles, Driver License Operations	P.O. Box 942890, Sacramento, CA 94290-0001	(916) 657-6525
COLORADO	Motor Vehicle Division, Driver Control Section	140 West 6th Avenue, Denver, CO 80204	(303) 205-5613
CONNECTICUT	Department of Motor Vehicles, Driver Services Division	60 State Street, Wethersfield, CT 06109	(860) 566-5250
DELAWARE	Division of Motor Vehicles, Driver Improvement Section	P.O. Box 698, Dover, DE 19903	(302) 739-4497
DISTRICT OF COLUMBIA	Bureau of Motor Vehicle Services, Traffic Records and Rehab Branch,	301 C Street NW, Washington, DC 20001	(202) 727-6761
FLORIDA	Bureau of Records	P.O. Box 5775, Tallahassee, FL 32314-5775	(904) 488-9145
GEORGIA	Department of Public Safety, Revocation Section	P.O. Box 1456, Atlanta, GA 30371	(404) 624-7561

STATE	AGENCY	ADDRESS	TELEPHONE
HAWAII	Motor Vehicle Safety Office	1505 Dillingham Blvd., Suite 214, Honolulu, HI 96817	(808) 832-5826
IDAHO	Motor Vehicle Bureau, Driver Services Section	P.O. Box 7129, Boise, ID 83707	(208) 334-8736
ILLINOIS	Department of Motor Vehicles, Driver Services Division	2701 South Dirksen Parkway, Springfield, IL 62723	(217) 785-1687
INDIANA	Bureau of Motor Vehicles, Safety Responsibility & Driver Improvement	State Office Building, Room 410, Indianapolis, IN 46204	(317) 232-2894
IOWA	Driver Records	100 Euclid, Park Fair Mall, P.O. Box 9204, Des Moines, IA 50306-9204	(515) 244-9124
KANSAS	Division of Vehicles, Driver Control & Licensing Bureau	Robert Docking State Office Building, Topeka, KS 66626	(913) 296-3671
KENTUCKY	Department of Vehicle Regulation, Division of Driver Licensing	State Office Building, 2nd Floor, Frankfort, KY 40622	(502) 564-6800
LOUISIANA	Department of Public Safety, Office of Motor Vehicles	P.O. Box 64886, Baton Rouge, LA 70896	(504) 925-3720
MAINE	Secretary of State, Motor Vehicle Division	State House, Station 29, August, ME 04333	(207) 287-2386
MARYLAND	Motor Vehicle Administration, Division of Driver Records	6601 Ritchie Highway NE, Glen Burnie, MD 21062	(410) 768-7659
MASSACHUSETTS	Registry of Motor Vehicles, Attn: Suspensions	1135 Tremont Street, Boston, MA 02120	(617) 351-7200
MICHIGAN	Department of State, Bureau of Driver and Vehicle Records	7064 Crowner Drive, Lansing, MI 48918	(517) 322-1571

STATE	AGENCY	ADDRESS	TELEPHONE
MINNESOTA	Driver & Vehicle Services Division	Transportation Building, Room 108, 395 John Ireland Blvd., St. Paul, MN 55155	(612) 297-2442
MISSISSIPPI	Department of Public Safety, Bureau of Driver Services,	P.O. Box 958 Jackson, MS 39205	(601) 987-1200
MISSOURI	Drivers License Bureau,	P.O. Box 200, Jefferson City, MO 65105	(573) 751-4475
MONTANA	Motor Vehicle Division, Driver Services Bureau, Driver Licensing Records Section	303 N. Roberts Street, Helena, MT 59620	(406) 444-4590
NEBRASKA	Department of Motor Vehicles, Driver Records Section	P.O. Box 94789, Lincoln, NE 68509	(402) 471-3985
NEVADA	Department of Motor Vehicles, Records Services Section	555 Wright Way, Carson City, NV 89711-0300	(702) 687-5505
NEW HAMPSHIRE	Division of Motor Vehicles, Records Section	James H. Hayes Safety Building, Hazen Drive, Concord, NH 03305	(602) 271-3109
NEW JERSEY	Division of Motor Vehicles, Driver Record Abstract Section	CN-142, 120 S. Stockton Street, Trenton, NJ 08666	(609) 292-6500
NEW MEXICO	Division of Motor Vehicles, Driver Services Bureau	P.O. Box 1028, Santa Fe, NM 87504-1028	(505) 827-0582
NEW YORK	Department of Motor Vehicles, Driver Licensing Division	Swan Street Building, Room 221, Empire State Plaza, Albany, NY 12228	(518) 474-0735
NORTH CAROLINA	Division of Motor Vehicles, Driver License Division	1100 New Bern Avenue, Raleigh, NC 27697	(919) 715-7000
NORTH DAKOTA	State Highway Department, Driver License & Traffic Safety Division	600 E. Boulevard Avenue, Bismarck, ND 58505	(701) 328-2603

STATE	AGENCY	ADDRESS	TELEPHONE
OHIO	Bureau of Motor Vehicles, Driver License Division	P.O. Box 16520, Columbus, OH 3266-0020	(614) 752-7500
OKLAHOMA	Department of Public Safety, Driver Improvement Bureau	P.O. Box 11415, Oklahoma City, OK 73136	(405) 425-2098
OREGON	Motor Vehicles Division, Driver Licensing Section	1905 Lana Avenue NE, Salem, OR 97314	(503) 945-5400
PENNSYLVANIA	Bureau of Driver Licensing, Information Sales Unit	P.O. Box 8691, Harrisburg, PA 17105	(800) 523-6429
RHODE ISLAND	Division of Motor Vehicles, Operator Control Section	345 Harris Avenue, Room 212, Providence, RI 02909	(401) 277-2994
SOUTH CAROLINA	South Carolina Department of Public Safety, Driver Records	P.O. Box 100178, Columbia, SC 29202-3178	(803) 251-2940
SOUTH DAKOTA	Department of Commerce & Regulation, Driver Improvement Program	118 W. Capitol Avenue, Pierre, SD 57501-2036	(605) 773-6883
TENNESSEE	Department of Safety, Driver Control Division	1150 Foster Avenue, Nashville, TN 37210	(615) 741-3954
TEXAS	Chief Department of Public Safety, Driver Improvement and Control	P.O. Box 4087, Austin, TX 78773	(512) 424-2600
UTAH	Motor Vehicle Division, Motor Vehicle Records Department	P.O. Box 30560, Salt Lake City, UT 84130-0560	(802) 965-4430
VERMONT	Department of Motor Vehicles, Driver Improvement	120 State Street, Montpelier, VT 05603	(802) 828-2050
VIRGINIA	Department of Motor Vehicles, Driver Licensing & Information Division	P.O. Box 27412, Richmond,VA 23269	(804) 367-0538
WASHINGTON	Department of Licensing, Division of Driver Services	Highways-Licenses Building, Olympia, WA 98504	(360) 902-3900

STATE	AGENCY	ADDRESS	TELEPHONE
WEST VIRGINIA	Department of Motor Vehicles, Driver Improvement Division	1800 Washington Street, East Charleston, WV 25317	(304) 558-0593
WISCONSIN	Department of Transportation, Compliance and Restoration Section	P.O. Box 7917, Madison, WI 53707	(608) 266-2261
WYOMING	Department of Transportation, Driver Control, Financial Responsibility Section	P.O. Box 1708, Cheyenne, WY 82003	(307) 777-4800

APPENDIX 7

INDIVIDUAL NDR FILE REQUEST FORM

Individual's Request for National Driver Register (NDR) File Check in Accordance with the Federal Privacy Act of 1974 (Public Law 93-579)

The National Driver Register (NDR) contains only a listing of names and related identification, provided by State driver licensing officials, of those drivers whose driver licenses have been cancelled, denied, revoked, or suspended or who have been convicted of certain serious traffic violations. The NDR does not contain a list of any other drivers. If you have *not* had a driver license cancelled, denied, revoked, or suspended or have *not* been convicted of serious traffic violations, you would not be listed in the NDR. Every individual is entitled, however, to request a check of the NDR records to determine whether they appear on the NDR file. The NDR will respond to every valid NDR inquiry.

The record content for those persons who are listed in the NDR files is limited to identification of the state(s) which have taken action to cancel, deny, revoke, or suspend or have records of conviction of serious traffic violations. Any specific information about the driver history, or the entire driver history, may be obtained only from the state(s) where the detailed information is recorded. The state(s) maintaining records are the (only) contacts able to correct records in error, and the NDR will correct its pointer records when so advised by a state indicating that a report previously made to the NDR is in error.

If the NDR has a record on you, the full record will be copied and sent to you including any older records which may have contained a reason for license cancellation, denial, revocation, or suspension. In addition, if such information has been disclosed by the NDR, the recipient of the information will also be identified.

The name and address of the State driver licensing official will be provided for each State listed as having reported information on you to the NDR.

Type or Print Plainly (Avoid delays. Inquiries that cannot be read will not be processed.)

Full Legal Name (First, Middle, and Last)				
Other Names Used (Maiden, Prior Name, Nickname, Professional Name, Other)				
Mailing Address: Number and Street with Apartment or Rural Route/Carrier & Box #			*Home Telephone (Optional)* Area Code Number ( )	
City, State and Zip Code			*Work Telephone (Optional)* Area Code Number ( )	
Driver License Number and State			*Soc. Security Number (Optional)*	
Month, Day, and Year of Birth	Sex	Color of Eyes	Height	Weight
Driver's Signature			Date	

NOTARIZATION

Notary Public
Stamp or Seal
(Mandatory)

Sworn to and ascribed before me

this ______ day of ____________

19________ in the city/county of

____

State of ____________________

How to Request an NDR Record Check

Any person may ask to know whether there is an NDR record on him or her and may obtain a copy of the record if one exists. That is the purpose for this form NDR-PRV. Complete the front side, have your signature (or your mark as witnessed) notarized, and mail the completed form to the National Driver Register at the address below.

The NDR response will be mailed to the mailing address shown, but incomplete or illegible inquiries will not be processed. All inquiries will be acknowledged if a return address is readable. Forms which are not notarized will also not be processed.

What to Expect from the NDR Record Check

The NDR will respond to every valid inquiry including requests which produce no record(s) on the NDR file. When records are located, details of the probable match results will be returned to the individual Privacy Act inquirer and will contain all information listed in the NDR records, if any, on the individual. The reply will also indicate any disclosures (reports to others) previously made by the NDR and will specify who, if anyone, has received reports on the inquirer.

Location of NDR Records

Records can be made available, within a reasonable time after request, for personal inspection and copying during regular working hours at 7:45 a.m. to 4:15 p.m., each day except Saturdays, Sundays, and Federal legal holidays. The address for requesting record information in writing directly from the NDR or for making requests in person is shown below.

APPENDIX 8

EMPLOYEE NDR FILE REQUEST FORM

Request for National Driver Register File Check on Current or Prospective Employee

Current or Prospective Employer to Receive the NDR Search Results: G Driver Employer G Railroad Company	
Employer or Agency Name	
To the specific attention of:	Business Telephone Area Code Number ( )
Mailing Address (Number and Street)	
City, State and Zip Code	

Type or Print Plainly (Avoid delays. Inquiries that cannot be read will not be processed.)				
Driver's Full Legal Name (First, Middle, and Last)				
Other Names Used (Maiden, Prior Name, Nickname, Professional Name, Other)				
Mailing Address (Number and Street with Apartment Number if any or Rural Route/Carrier and Box Number)			*Home Telephone (Optional)* Area Code Number ( )	
City, State and Zip Code			*Work Telephone (Optional)* Area Code Number ( )	
Driver License Number and State (Driver must be licensed in the state initiating the search)			*Social Security Number (Optional)*	
Month, Day, and Year of Birth	Sex	Color of Eyes	Height	Weight
EMPLOYEE UNDERSTANDING: I understand that the National Driver Register (NDR) search will result in a printed report which will be sent only to the employer or regulatory agency listed above on this form. The report will indicate either (1) that the NDR does **not** contain a record matching my identification *or* (2) that the NDR has a probable identification (match) from one state (or more) which will be named on the report. A separate check of state files would be required (1) to verify the identification or (2) to obtain the driving record. It is the responsibility of the listed employer to obtain the state driver records and to determine or verify records which apply to me. Under the Privacy Act, I have the right to request record(s) pertaining to me from the NDR. I also understand that if convictions, suspensions or revocations of mine are found which I have not shown on my applications or interviews, I might not be hired as a driver or could lose my job as a driver, and the State where I am licensed may also take action on my driver license including suspension, cancellation, or revocation. I hereby, with my signature, authorize a one-time file search of the NDR and any resulting reports to be sent to the employer or agency named on this form.				
Driver's Signature (Please read information on back before signing.)			Date	

<table>
<tr><td colspan="3">Official Use Only</td><td>NOTARIZATION
Required only if the NDR File Check Request is not made in person by the current or prospective operator.</td></tr>
<tr><td>Date Received</td><td>Date Sent</td><td>Internal Control</td><td rowspan="3">Sworn to and ascribed before me Notary Public
Seal or Stamp
this _______ day of ___________

19________ in the city/county of

____

State of ____________________</td></tr>
<tr><td colspan="3">TYPE OF IDENTIFICATION: G Valid Photo Driver License G StateBissued Photo ID
G Birth Certificate G Valid Passport G Valid Military ID
G Military Discharge Papers
G Other (specify) ____</td></tr>
<tr><td colspan="3">Employee Verifying Applicant Identification (Print Name) Signature</td></tr>
</table>

Requests for National Driver Register (NDR) Record Checks

Who May Obtain an NDR Record Check

Any person may ask to know whether there is an NDR record on him or her and may obtain a copy of the record if one exists. Requests from individuals require Form NDR-PRV.

Employers of drivers and locomotive engineers may also obtain NDR record checks. ***Every driver or operator on whom an NDR file check is requested is entitled to review the NDR report(s) provided to the employer.*** The results of the NDR check will be mailed only to the current or prospective employer. If no employer is named on the form or it is changed, the request will not be processed.

The following authorization applies to Railroad Company Requests

NDR CHECK AUTHORIZATION: The U. S. Department of Transportation, Federal Railroad Administration, in accordance with 49 CFR, Part 240.111, requires that I hereby request and authorize the National Highway Traffic Safety Administration (NHTSA) to perform an NDR check of my driving record for a 36-month period prior to the date of this request **including license withdrawal actions open at time of file check.** I hereby authorize the NDR to furnish a copy of the results of this NDR check directly to the railroad company identified on this inquiry form.

What NDR Records Contain

NDR results for employers will contain only the identification of the state(s) which have reported information on the driver to the NDR and only information reported within the past 3 years from the date of the inquiry. Driver control actions initiated prior to that time, even if still in effect, will not be included.

Detailed information to confirm identity or to describe the contents of the driver record can be obtained only from the State(s) listed when probable matches are reported. The name and address of the driver licensing official will be provided for each state listed.

How to Request an NDR Record Check

Using this form, which may be completed by either the current or prospective employer or the current or prospective employee, (1) the driver must authorize the request by his or her signature or mark as witnessed and (2) the driver must certify his or her identity.

Any mailed NDR record check request must be notarized to certify identity. Requests made in person require certification of identity acceptable to the state through one or more documents issued by a recognized organization (e.g., a driver's license or a credit card) which contains a means of verification such as a photograph or a signature.

Requests must be made to the state in which the driver is licensed.

Location of NDR Records

Records on individuals can be made available to those individuals, within a reasonable time after request, for personal inspection and copying during regular working hours at 7:45 a.m. to 4:15 p.m., each day except Saturdays, Sundays, and Federal legal holidays. The address for requesting record information in writing directly from the NDR or for making requests in person is C

National Driver Register
Nassif Building
400 7th Street, S.W.
Washington, DC 20590

APPENDIX 9:

NATIONAL HIGHWAY TRAFFIC AND SAFETY ADMINISTRATION (NHTSA) RECOMMENDATIONS ON CHILD SAFETY RESTRAINTS

Weight or Size of Child	Proper Type of Restraint
Children less than 20 pounds or less than 1 year	Rear-facing infant seat secured to the vehicle by the seat belts
Children from about 20 to 40 pounds and at least 1 year	Forward-facing child seat secured to the vehicle by the seat belts
Children more than 40 pounds	Booster seat, plus both portions of a lap/shoulder belt, except only the lap portion is used with some booster seats equipped with front shield.
Children who meet both of the following criteria below:	1) Their sitting height is high enough so that they can, without the aid of a booster seat, wear the shoulder belt comfortably across their shoulder and secure the lap belt across their pelvis; and (2) Their legs are long enough to bend over the front of the seat when their backs are against the vehicle seat back.

Note: Children should be placed in the backseat if possible. Consumers are also advised to check the child restraint manufacturer's recommendations concerning the weight of children who may safely use the restraint

Source: National Highway Traffic and Safety Administration (NHTSA).

APPENDIX 10

AIR BAG ON/OFF SWITCH REQUEST FORM

APPENDIX B TO PART 595--REQUEST FORM

U. S. DEPARTMENT OF TRANSPORTATION
NATIONAL HIGHWAY TRAFFIC SAFETY ADMINISTRATION

REQUEST FOR AIR BAG ON-OFF SWITCH

OMB. No. 2127-0588
Expiration Date: 11/30/00

Vehicle Owner or Lessee Instructions:

Read the National Highway Traffic Safety Administration (NHTSA) information brochure, "Air Bags & On-Off Switches, Information for an Informed Decision." If you want authorization for an on-off switch for your driver air bag, passenger air bag, or both, fill out Parts A, B, E and F completely, fill out Parts C and D as appropriate, and send this form to:

National Highway Traffic Safety Administration
Attention: Air Bag Switch Request Forms
400 Seventh Street, S. W.
Washington, D.C. 20590-1000

Please print.
Please note: Incomplete forms will be returned to the owner or lessee.
If you need a copy of the brochure or have any questions about how to fill out this form, call the NHTSA Hotline at 1-800-424-9393.

Part A. Name and address

____

(First) (Middle In.) (Last)

Residence: Street address City State Zip Code

Part B. I own or lease the following vehicle: (Owners of multiple vehicles should consult the additional instructions at the end of this form.)

Make Vehicle Identification Number
(located on driver's side of dashboard near windshield and on certification label on driver's door frame)

Model Model year

Part C. Switch for Driver Air Bag.

I request authorization for the installation of an on-off switch for the driver air bag in my vehicle. I certify that I or another driver of my vehicle meets the criteria for the risk group checked below.

(At least one box must be checked.)

☐ **Medical condition.** The driver has a medical condition which, according to his or her physician:

causes the driver air bag to pose a special risk for the driver; and
makes the potential harm from the driver air bag in a crash greater than the potential harm from turning off the air bag and allowing the driver, even if belted, to hit the steering wheel or windshield in a crash.

☐ **Distance from driver air bag.** Despite taking all reasonable steps to move back from the driver air bag, the driver is not able to maintain a 10-inch distance from the center of his or her breastbone to the center of the driver air bag cover.

Part D. Switch for Passenger Air Bag.

I request authorization for the installation of an on-off switch for the passenger air bag in my vehicle. I certify that I or another passenger of my vehicle meets the criteria for the risk group checked below.

(At least one box must be checked.)

Infant. An infant (less than 1 year old) must ride in the front seat because:

☐ my vehicle has no rear seat;
my vehicle has a rear seat too small to accommodate a rear-facing infant seat; or
the infant has a medical condition which, according to the infant's physician, makes it necessary for the infant to ride in the front seat so that the driver can constantly monitor the child's condition.

Child age 1 to 12. A child age 1 to 12 must ride in the front seat because:

☐ my vehicle has no rear seat;
although children ages 1 to 12 ride in the rear seat(s) whenever possible, children ages 1 to 12 sometimes must ride in the front because no space is available in the rear seat(s) of my vehicle; or
the child has a medical condition which, according to the child's physician, makes it necessary for the child to ride in the front seat so that the driver can constantly monitor the child's condition.

Medical condition. A passenger has a medical condition which, according to his or her physician:

☐ causes the passenger air bag to pose a special risk for the passenger; and
makes the potential harm from the passenger air bag in a crash greater than the potential harm from turning off the air bag and allowing the passenger, even if belted, to hit the dashboard or windshield in a crash.

Part E. I make this request based on following certification and understandings:

(Check each box below after reading carefully.)

☐ **Information brochure.** I certify that I have read the NHTSA information brochure, "Air Bags & On-Off Switches, Information for an Informed Decision." I understand that air bags should be turned off only for people at risk and turned back on for people not at risk.

☐ **Loss of air bag protection.** I understand that turning off an air bag may have serious safety consequences. When an air bag is off, even belted occupants may hit their head, neck or chest on the steering wheel, dashboard or windshield in a moderate to serious crash. That possibility may be increased in some newer vehicles with seat belts that are specially designed to work with the air bag. Those belts, which are designed to reduce the concentration of crash forces on any single part of the body, typically allow the occupant to move farther forward in a crash than older belts. Without the air bag to cushion this forward movement, the chance of the occupant hitting the vehicle interior is increased.

☐ **Waiver.** I understand that motor vehicle dealers and repair businesses may require me to sign a waiver of liability before they install an on-off switch.

Part F. Certification.

I certify to the U. S. Department of Transportation that the information, certifications and understandings given or indicated by me on this form are truthful, correct and complete to the best of my knowledge and belief. I recognize that the statements I have made on this form concern a matter within the jurisdiction of a department of the United States and that making a false, fictitious or fraudulent statement may render me subject to criminal prosecution under Title 18, United States Code, Section 1001.

Date Signature of owner/lessee

Additional instructions and information for vehicle owners and lessees: An owner or lessee of multiple vehicles (e.g., a fleet owner) who wants an on-off switch for the same air bag (e.g., just the passenger air bag) in more than one vehicle and for the same reason does not need to submit a separate form for each vehicle. Instead, the owner or lessee may list the make, model, model year, and vehicle identification number for each of those vehicles and attach the list to a copy of this form. Each page of the list must be signed and dated by the owner or lessee. A list may also be attached to a single copy of this form if the owner or lessee wishes to request authorization for on-off switches for both air bags in multiple vehicles.

Please note that an agency may not conduct or sponsor, and a person is not required to respond to, a collection of information unless it displays a currently valid OMB control number. That number appears above.

APPENDIX 11 :

DIRECTORY OF NHTSA REGIONAL OFFICES

REGION	ADDRESS	TELEPHONE	FACSIMILE	AREAS COVERED
NHTSA Region I	Transportation Systems Center, Kendall Square Code 903, Cambridge, MA 02142	617-494-3427	617-494-3646	CT, ME, MA, NH, RI, VT
NHTSA Region II	222 Mamaroneck Avenue, Suite 204, White Plains, NY 10605	914-682-6162	914-682-6239	NY, NJ, PR, VI
NHTSA Region III	10 South Howard Street, Suite 4000, Baltimore, MD 21201	410-962-0077	410-962-2770	DE, DC, MD, PA, VA, WV
NHTSA Region IV	61 Forsyth Street SW, Suite 17T30, Atlanta, GA 30303	404-562-3739	404-562-3763	AL, FL, GA, KY, MS, NC, SC, TN
NHTSA Region V	19900 Governors Drive, Suite 201, Olympia Fields, IL 60461	708-503-8822	708-503-8991	IL, IN, MI, MN, OH, WI
NHTSA Region VI	819 Taylor Street, Room 8a38, Fort Worth, TX 76102	817-978-3653	817-978-8339	AR, LA, NM, OK, TX, Indian N.
NHTSA Region VII	P.O. Box 412515 Kansas City, MO 64141	816-822-7233	816-822-2069	IA, KS, MO, NE
NHTSA Region VIII	555 Zang Street, Room 430, Denver, CO 80228	303-969-6917	303-969-6294	CO, MT, ND, SD, UT, WY
NHTSA Region IX	201 Mission Street, Suite 2230, San Francisco, CA 94105	415-744-3089	415-744-2532	AZ, CA, HI, NV, American Samoa, Guam, Mariana Islands

REGION	ADDRESS	TELEPHONE	FACSIMILE	AREAS COVERED
NHTSA Region X	3140 Jackson Federal Building, 915 Second Avenue, Seattle, WA 98174	206-220-7640	206-220-7651	AK, ID, OR, WA

APPENDIX 12:

STATE HELMET LAWS

STATE	MOTORCYCLE RIDERS COVERED	BICYCLE RIDERS COVERED	SEE FOOTNOTE
ALABAMA	all	younger than 16	n/a
ALASKA	17 and younger	n/a	1
ARIZONA	17 and younger	n/a	n/a
ARKANSAS	20 and younger	n/a	n/a
CALIFORNIA	all	younger than 18	n/a
COLORADO	n/a	n/a	n/a
CONNECTICUT	17 and younger	younger than 15	2
DELAWARE	18 and younger	younger than 16	2
DISTRICT OF COLUMBIA	all	n/a	n/a
FLORIDA	all	younger than 16	n/a
GEORGIA	all	younger than 16	n/a
HAWAII	17 and younger	n/a	n/a
IDAHO	17 and younger	n/a	n/a
ILLINOIS	n/a	n/a	n/a
INDIANA	17 and younger	n/a	2
IOWA	n/a	n/a	n/a
KANSAS	17 and younger	n/a	n/a
KENTUCKY	20 and younger	n/a	n/a
LOUISIANA	all	n/a	n/a
MAINE	14 and younger	n/a	3
MARYLAND	all	younger than 16	n/a
MASSACHUSETTS	all	younger than 13	4
MICHIGAN	all	n/a	n/a
MINNESOTA	17 and younger	n/a	2

STATE	MOTORCYCLE RIDERS COVERED	BICYCLE RIDERS COVERED	SEE FOOTNOTE
MISSISSIPPI	all	n/a	n/a
MISSOURI	all	n/a	n/a
MONTANA	17 and younger	n/a	n/a
NEBRASKA	all	n/a	n/a
NEVADA	all	n/a	n/a
NEW HAMPSHIRE	17 and younger	n/a	n/a
NEW JERSEY	all	younger than 14	n/a
NEW MEXICO	17 and younger	n/a	n/a
NEW YORK	all	younger than 14	4
NORTH CAROLINA	all	n/a	n/a
NORTH DAKOTA	17 and younger	n/a	5
OHIO	17 and younger	n/a	6
OKLAHOMA	17 and younger	n/a	n/a
OREGON	all	younger than 16	n/a
PENNSYLVANIA	all	younger than 12	n/a
RHODE ISLAND	20 years and younger	younger than 9	7
SOUTH CAROLINA	20 years and younger	n/a	n/a
SOUTH DAKOTA	17 and younger	n/a	n/a
TENNESSEE	all	younger than 16	n/a
TEXAS	20 years and younger	n/a	n/a
UTAH	17 and younger	n/a	n/a
VERMONT	all	n/a	n/a
VIRGINIA	all	n/a	n/a
WASHINGTON	all	n/a	n/a
WEST VIRGINIA	all	younger than 15	n/a
WISCONSIN	17 and younger	n/a	2
WYOMING	18 years and younger	n/a	n/a

Notes:

1. Alaska's motorcycle helmet use law covers passengers of all ages, drivers younger than 18, and drivers with instructional permits.

2. Motorcycle helmet laws in Connecticut, Delaware, Indiana, Minnesota and Wisconsin also cover drivers with instructional/learner's permits.

3. Maine's motorcycle helmet use law covers passengers 14 years and younger, drivers with learner's permits and drivers plus their passengers during the first year of licensure.

4. Bicycle helmet use laws in Massachusetts and New York prohibit people from transporting passengers younger than age 1.

5. North Dakota's motorcycle helmet use law covers all passengers traveling with drivers who are covered by the law.

6. Ohio's motorcycle helmet use law covers all drivers during the first year of licensure and all passengers of drivers who are covered by the law.

7. Rhode Island's motorcycle helmet use law covers all drivers during the first year of licensure.

Source: Insurance Institute for Highway Safety.

GLOSSARY

GLOSSARY

Appearance - To come into court, personally or through an attorney, after being summoned.

Arraign - In a criminal proceeding, to accuse one of committing a wrong.

Arraignment - The initial step in the criminal process when the defendant is formally charged with the wrongful conduct.

Arrest - To deprive a person of his liberty by legal authority.

Bail - Security, usually in the form of money, which is given to insure the future attendance of the defendant at all stages of a criminal proceeding.

Bail Bond - A document which secures the release of a person in custody, which is procured by security which is subject to forfeiture if the individual fails to appear.

Bench Warrant - An order of the court empowering the police or other legal authority to seize a person.

Burden of Proof - The duty of a party to substantiate an allegation or issue to convince the trier of fact as to the truth of their claim.

Capacity - Capacity is the legal qualification concerning the ability of one to understand the nature and effects of one's acts.

Cause of Action - The factual basis for bringing a lawsuit.

Civil Action - An action maintained to protect a private, civil right as opposed to a criminal action.

Civil Court - The court designed to resolve disputes arising under the common law and civil statutes.

Civil Law - Law which applies to non-criminal actions.

Civil Penalty - A fine imposed as punishment for a certain activity.

Confession - In criminal law, an admission of guilt or other incriminating statement made by the accused.

Court - The branch of government responsible for the resolution of disputes arising under the laws of the government.

Criminal Court - The court designed to hear prosecutions under the criminal laws.

Cross-Examination - The questioning of a witness by someone other than the one who called the witness to the stand concerning matters about which the witness testified during direct examination.

Culpable - Referring to conduct, it is that which is deserving of moral blame.

Damages - In general, damages refers to monetary compensation which the law awards to one who has been injured by the actions of another, such as in the case of tortious conduct or breach of contractual obligations.

Deductible - An amount an insured person must pay before they are entitled to recover money from the insurer, in connection with a loss or expense covered by an insurance policy.

Defendant - In a civil proceeding, the party responding to the complaint.

Defense - Opposition to the truth or validity of the plaintiff's claims.

District Attorney - An officer of a governmental body with the duty to prosecute those accused of crimes.

Docket - A list of cases on the court's calendar.

Due Process Rights - All rights which are of such fundamental importance as to require compliance with due process standards of fairness and justice.

Entrapment - In criminal law, refers to the use of trickery by the police to induce the defendant to commit a crime for which he or she has a predisposition to commit.

Exclusionary Rule - A constitutional rule of law providing that evidence procured by illegal police conduct, although otherwise admissible, will be excluded at trial.

Expert Witness - A witness who has special knowledge about a certain subject, upon which he or she will testify, which knowledge is not normally possessed by the average person.

Eyewitness - A person who can testify about a matter because of his or her own presence at the time of the event.

False Arrest - An unlawful arrest.

False Imprisonment - Detention of an individual without justification.

Family Purpose Doctrine - The doctrine which holds the owner of a family car liable in tort when it is operated negligently by another member of the family.

Featherbedding - An unfair labor practice whereby the time spent, or number of employees needed, to complete a particular task, is increased unnecessarily for the purpose of creating employment.

Felony - A crime of a graver or more serious nature than those designated as misdemeanors.

Finding - Decisions made by the court on issues of fact or law.

Forfeiture - The loss of goods or chattels, as a punishment for some crime or misdemeanor of the party forfeiting, and as a compensation for the offense and injury committed against the one to whom they are forfeited.

Hearing - A proceeding during which evidence is taken for the purpose of determining the facts of a dispute and reaching a decision.

Ignorantia Legis Non Excusat - Latin for "Ignorance of the law is no excuse." Although an individual may not think an act is illegal, the act is still punishable.

Illegal - Against the law.

Impound - To place property in the custody of an official.

Imprisonment - The confinement of an individual, usually as punishment for a crime.

Jail - Place of confinement where a person in custody of the government awaits trial or serves a sentence after conviction.

Judge - The individual who presides over a court, and whose function it is to determine controversies.

Jury - A group of individuals summoned to decide the facts in issue in a lawsuit.

Jury Trial - A trial during which the evidence is presented to a jury so that they can determine the issues of fact, and render a verdict based upon the law as it applies to their findings of fact.

Miranda Rule - The law requiring a person receive certain warnings concerning the privilege against self-incrimination, prior to custodial interrogation, as set forth in the landmark case of "Miranda v. Arizona."

Misdemeanor - Criminal offenses which are less serious than felonies and carry lesser penalties.

No Fault Laws - The insurance laws which provide compensation to any person injured as a result of an automobile accident, regardless of fault.

Offense - Any misdemeanor or felony violation of the law for which a penalty is prescribed.

Pain and Suffering - Refers to damages recoverable against a wrongdoer which include physical or mental suffering.

Plea Bargaining - The process of negotiating a disposition of a case to avoid a trial of the matter.

Probable Cause - The standard which must be met in order for there to be a valid search and seizure or arrest. It includes the showing of facts and circumstances reasonably sufficient and credible to permit the police to obtain a warrant.

Prosecution - The process of pursuing a civil lawsuit or a criminal trial.

Prosecutor - The individual who prepares a criminal case against an individual accused of a crime.

Public Defender - A lawyer hired by the government to represent an indigent person accused of a crime.

Search and Seizure - The search by law enforcement officials of a person or place in order to seize evidence to be used in the investigation and prosecution of a crime.

Summons - A mandate requiring the appearance of the defendant in an action under penalty of having judgment entered against him for failure to do so.

Trial - The judicial procedure whereby disputes are determined based on the presentation of issues of law and fact. Issues of fact are decided by the trier of fact, either the judge or jury, and issues of law are decided by the judge.

Verdict - The definitive answer given by the jury to the court concerning the matters of fact committed to the jury for their deliberation and determination.

Warrant - An official order directing that a certain act be undertaken, such as an arrest.

Warrantless Arrest - An arrest carried out without a warrant.

BIBLIOGRAPHY

BIBLIOGRAPHY

Black's Law Dictionary, Fifth Edition. St. Paul, MN: West Publishing Company, 1979.

Campbell, James F, Fisher, P. David and Mansfield, David A.*Defense of Speeding, Reckless Driving & Vehicular Homicide.* New York, NY: Mathew Bender, 1993 (Supp).

Insurance Institute for Highway Safety. (Date Visited: October 1998) http://www.hwysafety.org/.

Mothers Against Drunk Driving (M.A.D.D.). (Date Visited: October1998) http://www.madd.org/.

National Driver Register. (Date Visited: October 1998) http://www.nhtsa.dot.gov/people/perform/driver/.

National Highway Traffic Safety Administration. (Date Visited: October 1998) http://www.nhtsa.dot.gov/.

Office of the Assistant Secretary for Public Affairs. (Date Visited: October 1998) http://www.dot.gov/briefing.htm/.

United States Bureau of Transportation Statistics. (Date Visited: October 1998) http://www.bts.gov/.

United States Department of Transportation. (Date Visited: October 1998) http://www.dot.gov/.